GW01444925

Tigernán Ua Ruairc and a tw   *⌐ ⌐cus*

Maynooth Studies in Local History

SERIES EDITOR Raymond Gillespie

This year Maynooth Studies in Local History offers its usual, if slightly attenuated, selection of explorations of the local past. These four new volumes continue the tradition of their predecessors by interrogating the local historical experience of Ireland over a wide geographical and chronological range. In doing so they not only provide insights into the specifics of the local experience that is crucial to the understanding of the evolution of Irish society but they also reveal the infinite possibilities that the study of local history presents. Chronologically this year's group of small books range from a study of the implications of the 12th-century grant of land in what is now Co. Meath by Tigernán Ua Ruairc to the revelations thrown up by the activities of the rabble rouser and parricide John Linn in early 19th-century Belfast. These were undoubtedly very different worlds: the rolling plains of Meath as opposed to the grimy industrial world of a rapidly modernizing industrial city. The contrasts between these two places could not be greater but each study engages with these realities drawing evidence from the prestigious Book of Kells on the one hand and on the murky worlds documented in prison reports and parliamentary papers on the other. Both studies contribute to understanding the socially diverse worlds of the past and help shape how we understand the way in which those who inhabited them lived their daily lives.

These contrasts are even clearer in the other two studies included in this year's offering. We encounter the world of urban Ulster as seen through the eyes of those who lived in 17th- and 18th-century Belturbet juxtaposed with the rural society that developed on the Morristown Lattin estate in Kildare. The former was dominated by Protestant settlers who had arrived as part of the Plantation of Ulster whereas the latter was an estate owned by a Catholic landowner where both landlord and tenants struggled to find a way around the restrictive legislation on Catholic leasing and ownership of property. For all their contrasts these studies share a common theme – that of groups of people struggling to come terms with new and unexpected developments. These studies stretch the historical imagination beyond a mere chronicling of events within administrative or geographical boundaries and raise questions about why these diverse places have the personality that they have developed. They represent some of the most innovative and exciting research being undertaken in Irish history today and convey the vibrancy and excitement of the world of Irish local history.

Maynooth Studies in Local History: Number 145

Tigernán Ua Ruairc and a twelfth-century royal grant in the Book of Kells

Denis Casey

FOUR COURTS PRESS

Set in 10pt on 12pt Bembo by
Carrigboy Typesetting Services for
FOUR COURTS PRESS LTD
7 Malpas Street, Dublin 8, Ireland
www.fourcourtspress.ie
and in North America for
FOUR COURTS PRESS
c/o IPG, 814 N Franklin St, Chicago, IL 60610

ISBN 978–1–84682–858–4

Printed in Ireland
by SprintPrint, Dublin.

Contents

Acknowledgments

This book began as part of my PhD dissertation ('Studies in the exercise of royal power in Ireland, *c.*650–*c.*1200AD') submitted to the Department of Anglo-Saxon, Norse and Celtic (ASNC), University of Cambridge in 2009, in which I sought to explore the use of land (and particularly grants of land) by Irish kings, in order to contribute to our understanding of royal governance in Ireland. That original research was partly funded by a Robert Gardiner Memorial Scholarship at the University of Cambridge (2005–8) and the H.M. Chadwick Studentship fund (2008–9), for which I would like to record my gratitude.

My chief academic debt was (and in many respects still is) to my then supervisor, Prof. Máire Ní Mhaonaigh, for her advice, criticisms, encouragement and patience during that time, and her continued support afterwards. Like the good teacher in Kahlil Gibran's *The prophet*, she did not bid me enter the house of her wisdom, but rather led me to the threshold of my own understanding. I was also fortunate to be in a position to call upon the knowledge and advice of other members of the Department of ASNC and my Cambridge college, Trinity Hall, most notably Dr Geraldine Parsons (now at the University of Glasgow) and Dr Nigel Chancellor. In UCD, Dr Elva Johnston, Mr Charles Doherty and Prof. Michael Laffan of the School of History proved that I still had much to learn from them, even if I was no longer their student. Likewise, I gained much from the comments of my PhD examiners, Prof. Marie Therese Flanagan (formerly Queen's University Belfast) and Dr Fiona Edmonds (formerly Cambridge and now Lancaster University).

In preparing this volume for publication I would also like to thank the series editor Prof. Raymond Gillespie for accepting it and Dr Bernadette Cunningham of the Royal Irish Academy for her assistance. The cover image from Royal Irish Academy A v 3 is reproduced with the permission of the Royal Irish Academy. Likewise, I would like to thank Nick Maxwell of Wordwell for permission to adapt a map of Bréifne previously published in *History Ireland* for Figure 2.

My personal debts have only deepened in the intervening years. Firstly, I wish to thank my parents, James and Josephine Casey, without whose indefatigable support the original thesis would not have been possible; to them above all others this book is dedicated. My brother, Paul, and sister, Katie, were likewise unfailingly supportive and additions have thankfully been made to this list of supporters, most notably my sister-in-law, Eimear, and nephews, Seán and Michael. My work back then and in the intermediary period would not have been possible without the unstinting generosity and hospitality of my aunt Mary Conroy and her husband Eamonn, who treated me like a natural son, and the help of my friend and cousin, Rory Conroy. Sadly, but inevitably, there have been losses too, and – in the manner of D.A. Binchy's comments on his mentor Rudolf Thurneysen in his introduction to *Críth Gablach* – it is a melancholy reflection that a work that should have been dedicated to my grand-aunt, Kitty Spillane, is now inscribed to her memory.

Good friends around the globe have been there for me through bad times and good, and I hope nobody is offended if I restrict myself to naming four and their families: Helen Hannigan, Pat O'Sullivan, Rosie Bonté and Line Espedal. Few people in the world could say they have had such an assemblage of friends; none can know my debts and the depths of affection I hold for them.

Introduction

In an age when kings could be inaugurated in the morning and knifed and buried by sundown, Tigernán Ua Ruairc's 50-year reign over Bréifne (*c.*1122–72) is worthy of note for its longevity alone. Yet durability was but one of his many accomplishments, for in that time he oversaw his kingdom's transformation from regional power to national player and his influence broke and made the last two high-kings of Ireland, Muirchertach Mac Lochlainn (*ob.*1166) and Ruaidrí Ua Conchobair (*ob.*1198). Little wonder that Irish annalists chronicling the passing of the centuries could look back upon him (on his death in 1172) as 'a man of great power for a long time'.[1]

Ua Ruairc was remarkably successful in expanding the borders of Bréifne (from its heartlands in modern Co. Cavan) at the expense of the Uí Maíl Shechnaill rulers of the kingdom of Mide (modern counties Meath, Westmeath and Longford), whose terminal decline began in the 11th century. In looking at how Ua Ruairc was able to redraw the political map to his own advantage, we are fortunate that among a series of short land transaction documents originally recorded in the Book of Kells (sometimes erroneously dubbed 'charters') two issued by Tigernán survive. Surprisingly, given the paucity of such sources surviving from medieval Ireland, these documents have only received modest scrutiny. Merely 12 such *notitiae* (singular *notitia*) – 'notes' recording land transactions normally drawn up by one of the participants – written between 1033 and 1161 survive from Kells (which is by far the largest corpus among the 18 surviving examples).[2] They were entered into the blank spaces and margins of the 9th-century Book of Kells (one of the most famous manuscripts surviving from medieval Europe), which was then considered a relic of the 6th-century saint Columba (Irish Colum Cille, *ob.*595/7), the patron of the church of Kells and of a wider Columban *familia* (an association of churches, literally 'family').[3]

As Marie Therese Flanagan has noted, 'although it can be suggested that in one way those insertions were intended to invest the property rights with the permanency of divine sanction, at another level there is something shocking about this splendidly illuminated gospel text, so precious that it had been provided with a decorated protective case (*cumdach*), being used as a register for mundane land transactions'.[4] Indeed it might seem like an act of vandalism to modern eyes to have treated the magnificent Book of Kells in this way, but to medieval eyes the margins of manuscripts were the accepted place for interacting with the text and could be something of a public forum.[5] One of these insertions in particular, which records the granting of a substantial area of land known as Mag nDechrad ('Plain of Dechrae') to the church of Kells (*c*.1152), is the subject of this book. Regardless of sanctity or profanity, it offers a valuable insight into the *modus operandi* of a remarkably successful king, while also contributing to our knowledge of the greater Kells area on the eve of the English invasion.

Study of medieval Irish kingship has all too often focused on ideology (e.g., concepts such as *fír flathemon* ('prince's truth')), to the neglect of more mundane matters, and we still labour under the influence of outdated and ridiculous notions, such as early Irish kings symbolically marrying 'sovereignty goddesses' (a supposed goddess who personifies the concept of sovereignty and by extension the land – but which is in reality an early 20th-century scholarly construct). Historians of medieval Ireland have too often focused their attention on esoteric features of Irish kingship, such as the possible survival of aspects of pre-Christian ideology and practices, and the study of such facets of kingship, while not without its value, has occurred at the expense of investigating the practical challenges of everyday royal rule. As Patrick Wormald pointed out: 'historians of kingship have arguably been too preoccupied by ideology, especially if the ideology is in any way weird. All societies have their political rhetoric, and its study is both legitimate and necessary; but it is never the whole story'.[6] Thus while much has been written about ideological constructs, historians still remain very much in the dark about basic aspects of royal rule. Consequently, examining Ua Ruairc's grant of Mag nDechrad to the church of Kells offers the opportunity to observe how kings engaged in practical administrative matters that had political, ecclesiastical and military significance, offering insights into how medieval Irish rulers exercised their power rather than how it was conceptualized.

By focusing upon a grant of land, this study also offers an opportunity to contribute to local history through suggesting a location and extent of Mag nDechrad (which has not previously been attempted). In addition, the grant's guarantor list may be read as a *who's who* of grandees and interested parties, enabling us to see who moved in the corridors of power and had particular interests in western Co. Meath during the middle of the 12th century. More broadly it sheds light on those areas that constituted the overkingdoms of Bréifne and Mide in the same period (Cavan, Leitrim, Longford, Westmeath and particularly Meath), shortly before the English conquests altered the political landscape to enduring effect.

In order to achieve these aims, this book begins with an overview of medieval Irish attitudes to land and the importance they attached to it, seeking to place the subsequent large donations of Tigernán Ua Ruairc in perspective (first chapter). Possession and exploitation of land were central to both the exercise and ideological construction of kingship, and yet land alienation was, paradoxically, a key weapon in the political arsenal of resourceful kings like Ua Ruairc. From there, both the donor (Ua Ruairc) and the recipient (the church of Kells) will be subject to a brief overview (second chapter), followed by a discussion of the corpus of *notitiae* in the Book of Kells and how scholars have interpreted them as legal documents and sources of social history (third chapter). The longest section (fourth chapter) is reserved for an analysis of the 1152 *notitia*, exploring the reasons and contexts for the grant, who was involved and the extent of the territory donated.

The *notitia* recording the grant of Mag nDechrad to Kells stands at the confluence of the local, national and international. While ostensibly recording a transfer of land ownership in Co. Meath, it may well have been executed in conjunction with the Synod of Kells (1152), an enormous gathering presided over by a papal cardinal-legate, which sought to align the structure of the Irish church more closely with Continental norms, and as such this *notitia* may be read in the context of the church reform movement that played such a prominent part in the history of western Europe during the 11th and 12th centuries.

1. Land in medieval Ireland

Irish obsession with land ownership did not begin with John B. Keane's *The Field* and the overwhelmingly rural character of medieval Irish society ensured that control of land (particularly agriculturally productive land) was a key feature in the accumulation of wealth and power. According to Old Irish legal texts (dating mainly from the 7th to 9th centuries), land was so central to wealth and status that even the possession of cattle – the currency of so many medieval transactions – was inferior to land. *Ferr mruig mlichtaib* ('land is better than milkings') the wise king Flann Fína (*ob*.705) is supposed to have pronounced.[1] Unsurprisingly, a keen eye for agrarian practicalities glares out from many texts, as is evident in the detailed analysis of land values and factors affecting productivity in the 8th-century law text *Tír Cumaile* ('Land of a Cumal').[2] So extensive is the treatment accorded to ownership and agricultural exploitation of land, in this and other 7th- and 8th-century law texts, that they are sufficient to enable a detailed reconstruction of early Irish farming.[3]

In such an agrarian society, acquisition and loss of land made and broke men. A freeman lost his standing through dissipating his holdings, while an outsider could gain legal status within a *túath* ('petty kingdom') by purchasing land.[4] The 9th-century *Triads* (nuggets of wisdom arranged in threes) cast landownership as a dividing line between aristocratic status and servility; a lord who sold his land made a slave of himself.[5] While undoubtedly an exaggeration, the point is clear: it was eminently preferable to maintain one's holdings than to dispose of them. The church too shared a preoccupation with proprietorship, and the large corpus of saints' Lives, from as early as the 7th-century Latin Lives of St Patrick to 12th-century vernacular Lives, bears ample witness to this. A notable example of the latter is *Betha Cholmáin meic Lúacháin* ('The Life of Colmán mac Lúacháin') of Lann, Co. Westmeath, which is almost a hagiographic cartulary (register of charters) of the lands claimed by Colmán's ecclesiastical heirs in the 12th century (and roughly contemporary with Tigernán Ua Ruairc's reign).[6]

Prime agricultural land has the ability to provide sustenance for more people per acre than more unproductive areas, which in turn resulted in kingdoms that occupied fertile regions possessing larger populations. A large population has, as a natural corollary, a bigger potential workforce and military and tax-paying capacity, while greater population density ensures easier lines of communication, allowing for quicker mobilization of these forces. Thus it is unsurprising to find that for much of medieval Irish history the well-drained fertile soils of the midland plains were home to the powerful dynasties of Clann Cholmáin in Mide (Co. Westmeath) and Síl nÁeda Sláine in Brega (counties Meath and Dublin), an area that jointly became subsumed under the name of Mide by the 12th century. In contrast boggy, poorly-drained uplands were often occupied by politically insignificant peoples, such as the Corco Duibne in west and south-west Kerry. This pattern can even be seen in individual kingdoms that contained districts of differing productivity, for example Tír Conaill. Mag Serid (a fertile area in the south of modern Co. Donegal) was the home of the Uí Chanannáin and Uí Maíl Doraid kings of Tír Conaill for much of its history,[7] which may be contrasted with the largely mountainous areas of poor-quality soil in the north of the kingdom, which were the home of the less successful Cenél Lugdach. Even Cenél Lugdach were located primarily in a small area of productive land along the Glenna river valley between the 6th and 9th centuries.[8]

The possession of large areas of agriculturally productive land, however, may not always have been the deciding factor in power politics. Strategic location of kingdoms may also have played a part. For example, the position of Dál Cais (and subsequently Uí Briain) in the Shannon basin aided their dominance of the Viking town of Limerick and their rise to power in the late 10th century.[9] Nonetheless, the possession of productive land may have been critical for sustained power, hence the Eóganacht of south Munster, who occupied some of the best land in Ireland, were able to withstand Dál Cais pressure and revive their fortunes in the 12th century.[10] It is doubtless more than coincidental that later great Anglo-Norman lordships were based in the productive lands previously held by powerful Irish dynasties, for example the earls of Kildare held much of the territory previously possessed by Uí Dúnlainge kings of Laigin (Leinster), while the de Lacy lordship of Meath was carved out of Mide and Brega.

REASONS FOR ALIENATING LAND

Given this emphasis on land acquisition and retention, Tigernán Ua Ruairc's granting away of Mag nDechrad to Kells might seem counter-intuitive. Why would an expansionist king like Ua Ruairc be willing to part with so substantial an area as Mag nDechrad? Reasons for, and modes of transferring land were quite varied, including selling land, periodic redistribution of jointly-owned kinland among kin members, granting land as a fief to a client, contracting marriages, and overlords displacing lesser peoples in order to give their holdings to supporters, to name but some. Among such contexts, land offered as compensation for crimes or as gestures of atonement/goodwill and pious donations to the church are perhaps the most relevant to Tigernán's career.

Annals, literary sources and records of land transactions suggest that land was sometimes surrendered by kings to atone for crimes they had committed, often to the church. For example, in the early 9th century the king of Uí Maine (south

Roscommon and south-east Galway) drowned the vice abbot of Clonmacnoise and seven churches were granted to the community of Clonmacnoise in recompense.[11] The details of this grant have not survived and it is uncertain what its conditions entailed; it may have been a complete and unconditional alienation of those churches and their property, or simply a surrender of certain rights over them to Clonmacnoise that were previously held by the king of Uí Maine. Similarly, the Céli Dé (houses of strict observance) at Clonmacnoise and Clondalkin (Co. Dublin) were the recipients of two land grants in reparation for outrages during the 11th century,[12] while in the 12th century an assassination in Derry was substantially compensated for with cattle, promise of service to the monastic community, and land.[13]

The practice of atonement through land offerings also appears to have had literary reflexes. According to two 12th-century texts, *Lebor na Cert* ('The Book of Rights') and *Aided Crimthainn meic Fhidaig* ('The violent death of Crimthann son of Fidach'), in the distant past the kingdom of Osraige (mainly modern Co. Kilkenny) is said to have been given to Munster by the Laigin (Leinstermen) as an *éraic* (a fine for homicide), in reparation for the slaying of the king of Munster.[14] In this instance, rather than record an actual transaction, the depiction of the transfer of a whole kingdom suggests that the concept was used to justify contemporary Munster political ambitions to dominate Osraige (one king of which, Donnchad mac Gilla Pátraic (*ob.*1039), actually took the kingship of Laigin in the 11th century).[15] However, as is evident from the *notitia* that records Conchobor ua Maíl Shechnaill's 11th-century grant to the church of Kildalkey, even such acts of restitution could be manipulated by the offending parties for political ends,[16] and the same might be said of the first of Tigernán Ua Ruairc's two surviving Kells *notitiae*, which records a grant to the church of Int Ednén (Inan, south-west Meath), between 1122 and 1148.[17]

A considerable number of sources (for example hagiography, charters and annals) depict kings presenting land or rights over land to churches, and in the hagiographic tradition this often involved the portrayal of an individual promising land to a saint in return for some special favour or in atonement for a wrong inflicted upon that saint. Such incidents may have been invented to emphasize the obligations of the descendants of the supposed donor to the church of the saint and to stress the benefits of such a relationship, namely the assurance of divine favour. Genuine religious fervour may have played a part in some grants, for example in 1096 fear of divine retribution resulted in numerous offerings (including lands) to churches.[18] Demonstration of regal might and largesse may also have been a factor, as when the high-king Muirchertach Mac Lochlainn granted land to the clergy of Sabal (Saul, Co. Down) *tria rath righi h-Uí Lochlainn* ('by reason of the prosperity of the reign of Ua [Mac] Lochlainn'), after he inflicted two humiliating defeats upon the Ulaid (Ulstermen) in a single year (1165).[19] Similarly, the use of land donation as a means to express political power is a motif that comes across in Tigernán Ua Ruairc's 12th-century grants to Kells.

THE SOCIAL CONTEXT OF GRANTS: RECIPROCITY

When considering gifts of property and property rights to the church, such as those by Tigernán Ua Ruairc, modern concepts of gift giving should not tempt us to think that such donations were unilateral. In modern perception gift giving is a casual occurrence, often performed in friendship, which does not create a formal relationship. In contrast, as Charles Doherty has noted, medieval gift giving was a formalized process intended to forge binding social and political ties, and acceptance of a gift required a commensurate response.[20] This concept appears to have functioned at all levels of society. Just as gift giving between free individuals bound them together, so too the collection and distribution of tribute by the church or kings bound them to the populace. Gift giving not only forged links but was an essential part of status. In early legal texts, such as the 7th-/8th-century *Críth Gablach*, kingship was regarded as a reciprocal contract whereby, as Thomas Charles-Edwards has summarized, 'the king's rights were the consideration which answered his obligations and his obligations were the consideration for his rights'.[21] Similar to a king, the status of a *flaith* ('lord') was based on his reciprocal relationship with his subordinates. The *flaith*'s subordinates (his clients) each received a *rath* ('fief') from him, in exchange for reciprocal dues.[22] Likewise, the church was obliged to provide religious services in return for dues from the population, default on which resulted in loss of status. The 8th-century *Ríagail Pátraic* ('The Rule of Patrick') claims that a church could not expect to profit from its tenants unless it reciprocated by providing baptism, communion and intercession for the dead. The term used in this text to describe the relationship is *frithfholad* ('mutual/counter obligations'),[23] which also occurs in an 8th-/9th-century text on the reciprocal relationship between the kings of Munster and their client kings.[24] The fullest expression of the importance of the exchange of gifts and the social bonds they created is found in the 11th-/12th-century *Lebor na Cert*, which contains a local and national schema for the reciprocal rights and dues of the kings of Ireland.[25]

Notwithstanding these deeply-embedded social behavioural patterns, the provision of land by a secular ruler or individual to a church (as depicted in the hagiography, *notitiae* and later charters) may have occasionally been pietistic or at least have had a genuine religious element. A *quid pro quo* relationship, however, may have been much closer to the norm and donors may have retained a vested interest in land granted. Such reciprocal rights may have included the important right to billet soldiers on churches. One of the most detailed treatments of billeting is found in a later poem in the longer of the two Irish Lives of Máedóc, the supposed founder of Ferns (Co. Wexford) and patron of Drumlane (Co. Cavan), which was favoured by Uí Ruairc. One stanza, which is said to have been uttered by the *comarba* (ecclesiastical successor, lit. 'heir') of Máedóc, suggests some of the complexities of the billeting process:

Cion do chur i n-Druim Lethan
do rioghaibh mar gnathachadh,
ni thiubhar amach go brath,
ar connradh creach na conách.

To impose a levy on Drumlane
as a customary due to kings,
I will never concede until [the day of] judgment,
for treaty of spoils, or wealth.[26]

Not only might kings expect billeting rights as a customary due, but churches might also have benefited from the system by receiving a portion of the spoils which kings might accumulate. This suggests that the exercise of billeting may have been performed in a directly transactional manner, in addition to being a consequence of previous church endowment (the latter is suggested in a mid-12th-century *notitia* concerning Cenél Lóegaire's billeting rights at the church of Ardbraccan, Co. Meath).[27] A church receiving a donation from a shrewd king might end up with more than it bargained for (literally or metaphorically), and Tigernán Ua Ruairc was one of the most cunning men in 12th-century Ireland.

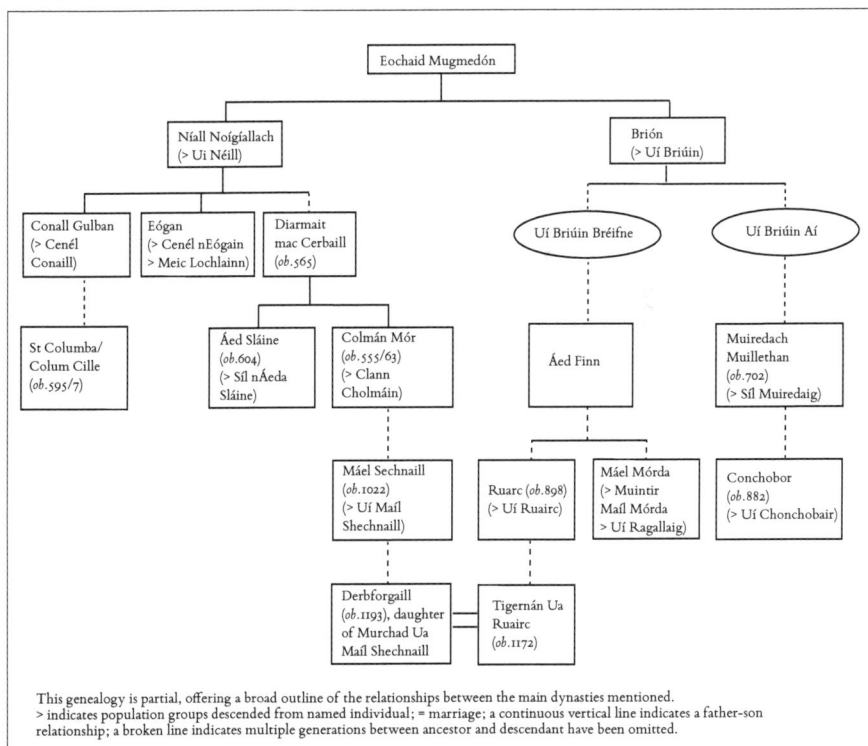

This genealogy is partial, offering a broad outline of the relationships between the main dynasties mentioned.
> indicates population groups descended from named individual; = marriage; a continuous vertical line indicates a father-son relationship; a broken line indicates multiple generations between ancestor and descendant have been omitted.

1. Genealogy of Uí Néill and Uí Briúin.

2. Tigernán Ua Ruairc and the church of Kells

Few medieval Irish kings could boast of being as successful and as long-lived as Tigernán Ua Ruairc (*ob*.1172), although he is now chiefly remembered for his conflict with Diarmait Mac Murchada (*ob*.1171), king of Laigin (Leinster), after Mac Murchada kidnapped Tigernán's wife Derbforgaill (daughter of Murchad Ua Maíl Shechnaill, king of Mide) in 1152, which various later (and somewhat biased) sources suggest was the cause of the coming of the English to Ireland.[1] The annalists who cursed him during his early career for attacking the retinue of the *comarba Pátraic* (head of the church of Armagh) were forced to concede that by its end he was a *fer cumachta more fhri ré fhota* ('a man of great power for a long time'),[2] whose dynasty had emerged from Bréifne – unappealingly known as one of the *trí haimréide hÉrenn* ('three rough places of Ireland')[3] – to sit at the top table of Irish politics. A whiff of mystery surrounds how they did so, as the earliest members of Uí Briúin Bréifne (his dynasty) in the annalistic record are obscure and the Uí Briúin Bréifne genealogical pedigree was clearly forged to give them a more illustrious background than they possessed, and to create a link between them and the Uí Briúin rulers of Connacht (see Fig. 1).[4] Even Tigernán's immediate ancestry is unclear. In his grant to the church of Int Ednén (which appears to predate his grant of Mag nDechrad to Kells), Tigernán is named as the son of Áed, son of Domnall Ua Ruairc, yet the brief (almost contemporary) 12th-century pedigree of Uí Briúin Bréifne found in the Book of Leinster names Tigernán's father as Donnchad, son of Domnall.[5]

If historians have trouble knowing where Tigernán came from, his contemporaries found it equally difficult to know where he was going. He appears in the historical record as an arch-opportunist who repeatedly changed sides in the 12th-century's endemic political and military struggles, a characteristic he shared with other contemporary Irish kings, such as his father-in-law Murchad Ua Maíl Shechnaill of Mide (*ob*.1153), and it has been estimated that he changed his political allegiances approximately 16 times during his career prior to the coming of the English (*c*.1124–69).[6] During that period his chief aims appear to have been survival within Bréifne and expansion of its southern borders. He was enormously successful in dominating Mide over almost half a century, and it is not unreasonable to assume that occasional allocations of portions of Mide to Tigernán, by the Uí Chonchobair and Meic Lochlainn claimants to the high kingship, were partly in recognition of his existing control over large swathes of its territory.

Such was his dominance that Gerald of Wales, writing in the 1180s, entitled Ua Ruairc king of Mide, although this perspective was not universal.[7] The Norman-French poem known as *The song of Dermot and the Earl*, composed mainly in the last decade of the 12th century, did not consider him so, but nevertheless acknowledged him as one of the most powerful kings in Ireland.[8] Still, a measure of the success Tigernán and his uterine half-brother Donnchad Ua Cerbaill of Airgialla (*ob*.1168) had in making inroads upon Mide can be discerned in Henry II's later grant of Mide to Hugh de Lacy. The extent of the territory granted to de Lacy was that held previously by Murchad Ua Maíl Shechnaill.[9] Murchad had died 18 years prior to the arrival of Henry and Mide must have lost so much territory to its neighbours between 1153 and 1172 that it was necessary to use Murchad's kingdom (rather than the contemporary Uí Maíl Shechnaill-controlled rump) as the basis of an adequate grant to de Lacy.

Political fickleness, coupled with his success in absorbing Uí Maíl Shechnaill territory, marks out Tigernán as one of the most successful practitioners of *realpolitik* in 12th-century Ireland, and the *notitia* recording Tigernán's grant of Mag nDechrad to Kells offers a fascinating insight into the *modus operandi* of a politically savvy and ambitious king.[10]

KELLS — *ÁINIUS HÉRENN* ('THE SPORT OF IRELAND')[11]

The beneficiary of Tigernán's largesse, the church of Kells, lay in the plain of Brega, which stretched from the river Liffey at Dublin to the hills of south Co. Louth, an area drained primarily by the rivers Boyne and Blackwater and containing some of the most productive agricultural land in Ireland.[12] The Blackwater valley (in modern Co. Meath) was the location of a number of important secular and ecclesiastical sites in pre-Norman Ireland. Among those clustered along a mere 20km of the Blackwater's banks are Ráith Airthir (an important seat of Síl nÁeda Sláine kingship during the late 7th and early 8th centuries), Tailtiu (the site of the Uí Néill's communal gathering known as *Óenach Tailten*), Domnach Pátraic (one of the earliest churches to be named after St Patrick), Tuilén (Dulane, where the 9th-century prologue to the great law collection known as the *Senchas Már* may have been written)[13] and Kells.[14] This area's importance, as Catherine Swift has argued convincingly, is demonstrated by the struggles for dominance among the warring factions of the then powerful Síl nÁeda Sláine, which were fought out in this valley during the late 7th and early 8th centuries.[15] Thus the Blackwater valley, in which Kells is located, formed an important sphere of interest for the dominant branch of the Southern Uí Néill of the time, who were also claimants to and occasional holders of the kingship of Tara.

THE STATUS OF PRE-COLUMBAN KELLS

The status of Kells prior to the arrival of the Columban *familia* is uncertain, but later sources depict it possessing regal associations stretching back into prehistory. Laigin-orientated texts (particularly the early Middle Irish tale *Esnada Tige Buchet* and genealogical material relating to the descendants of the important ancestor figure Fíachu Ba hAiccíd) claim that the mythical kings Cormac mac Airt and Conn Cétchathach resided at Kells, both of whom were ancestors of the Uí Néill and Connachta (including Uí Briúin Bréifne).[16] A short Middle Irish text that also displays Laigin bias, *Fotha Catha Cnucha*, claims that while Cathaír Már – a pivotal Laigin ancestor figure – was king of Tara, Conn Cétchathach was *hi Cenandos hi ferand rigdomna* ('in Kells in the *rígdomna*'s land').[17] The term *rígdomna*, often translated as 'royal heir', might best be understood as 'one who was worthy of being king', and could also be applied to dynasts of high standing who were not expected to succeed to the kingship. Either way, there was a clear attempt to link Kells with the regal prestige of Tara.

Not only were all these kings unhistorical but the sources referring to them were all composed after the construction of the Columban church at Kells in the first decade of the 9th century, and were part of an effort to back-project onto Kells a regal history that it did not possess. The first historical king to be associated with Kells was Diarmait mac Cerbaill (*ob.*565), and even this link is dubious. Diarmait is a figure much encrusted with legend and his connection with Kells was probably as fictitious as that of Cormac or Conn. Kells is described as Diarmait's *prímdún* ('chief fort') in the Middle Irish tale *Aided Bresail* (in which he kills his own son, but is forgiven through the good offices of Columba),[18] while the 12th-century Middle Irish Life of Columba claims that Columba and the prophet Bec mac Dé both prophesied to another of Diarmait's sons, Áed Sláine (eponymous ancestor of Síl nÁeda Sláine), that Diarmait's fortress at Kells would one day become a Columban church.[19]

F.J. Byrne offered an attractive reason for viewing Kells as an existing royal site at the time of its foundation in the early 9th century, after the Columban *familia*'s headquarters on the island Iona (western Scotland) had suffered severely from the Vikings. To Byrne, 'that Kells itself should have been a royal site affords a striking parallel to the apparently contemporaneous foundation of a safer inland metropolis for the Columban community in Scotland at Dunkeld'.[20] Unfortunately this parallel with Dunkeld (originally a Pictish royal foundation) is quite circumstantial, and the only reliable evidence for pre-Columban Kells is Tírechán's claim in the late 7th century (over a century prior to the Columban foundation), that there was a church *iuxta Cenondas* ('beside Kells').[21] In short, since the majority of the sources for Kells' pre-Columban period were composed after the founding of the Columban church, and concern themselves with people of doubtful historicity, there does not appear to be any reason to accept the validity of the notion that Kells was a pre-Columban royal site.[22]

LAND DONATION AS A POLITICAL TOOL IN THE FOUNDING OF KELLS

By the early 9th century (when the Columban church at Kells was founded), the tactic of kings granting away land in subject kingdoms in order to reduce the power of their subordinates appears to have been already well-established in Ireland. The foundation of another venerable Columban church, Durrow, may have been the result of such a practice.[23] Durrow was located in the Southern Uí Néill kingdom of Cenél Fíachach (Co. Offaly) but was founded by Columba himself, a saint of a Northern Uí Néill kingdom, Cenél Conaill (Co. Donegal). Columba may have founded Durrow with the aid of his powerful kinsman and then Cenél Conaill king of Tara, Áed mac Ainmirech (*ob*.598), who as king of Tara held a position of prominence among the Northern and Southern Uí Néill power blocs. A number of other important churches such as Birr, Kinnitty, Lynally, Rahugh and Rahan were located in Cenél Fíachach, yet many of their patron saints, for example Colmán of Lynally and Áed mac Bricc of Rahugh, were associated with Uí Néill generally and not Cenél Fíachach.[24] The profusion of ecclesiastical establishments in Cenél Fíachach resulted in its border with Munster eventually obtaining the moniker *Tír Chell* ('land of churches').[25] It may be no coincidence that, although Fíachu (eponym of Cenél Fíachach) was one of the chief agents of Uí Néill expansion during the early decades of the 6th century, his descendants were not in contention for the kingship of Tara by the end of that century.[26] Their land may have been consumed by the flourishing of churches in their territory, as Birr, Rahugh and Rahan (and possibly Kinnitty and Lynally too) had been founded in Cenél Fíachach by the end of the 6th century.[27]

Charles Doherty, however, has suggested another way of interpreting grants of land to the church in subject kingdoms. Using the example of a 7th-century grant of land to the church of Balla, by the Connacht dynasty Uí Fhíachrach, he has suggested that the initiative may have lain with the weaker group – 'it is particularly important to note the magnanimity of the dynasty that is rapidly losing power. Giving land to the church was one way of preventing it from falling into the hands of one's opponents'.[28] Following this theory, it is reasonable to suppose that dynasties in decline may have accelerated the corrosion of their own secular power by means of such grants. If the donor's dynasty subsequently supplied the ruling personnel of the recipient church the net loss of land would have been minimal, and power preserved through diversifying its interests. These interpretations of gifts of property to churches in subordinate kingdoms are not necessarily mutually exclusive, and could have been at work at the same time.

Despite the later accretion of tradition regarding the status of pre-Columban Kells, the surrounding area was nevertheless important during the 8th century, prior to the founding of its Columban church. The two main Southern Uí Néill dynastic groups, Clann Cholmáin and Síl nÁeda Sláine, both claimed descent from the shadowy 6th-century Diarmait mac Cerbaill, and as Clann Cholmáin grew in power during the 8th century (at the expense of the internally divided Síl nÁeda Sláine), the area around Kells became both an issue of contention and a battleground between these two factions, just as it had previously been among branches of Síl nÁeda Sláine. The area was the meeting place of a number of bordering kingdoms (such as Fir Cúil Breg, Uí Macc Uais Breg, Luigne and Uí Beccon), which both Clann Cholmáin rulers of Mide and Síl nÁeda Sláine rulers of Brega sought to control.[29]

It was within this political context that the Columban community established the church of Kells in this area in the first decade of the 9th century.[30] The morphology of that *nova civitas* ('new city') is possibly reflected in the street pattern of modern Kells (which indicates that the outer enclosure surrounded an area of 9.5 hectares or twenty-two acres), but beyond that the features of the early church site are difficult to discern.[31] It has been suggested that Kells may have originally been intended as a place of refuge for the monks of Iona from Viking attacks and eventually became the new headquarters of the Columban *familia*.[32] Although Iona undoubtedly suffered from Viking attacks prior to the construction of Kells, it is not certain that the latter was founded expressly for the purpose of refuge.[33] If it was, then it is somewhat anomalous that not only was a Columban presence maintained on Iona, but that Iona appears to have retained the leadership of the Columban *familia* for some time afterwards.[34] Nonetheless, even if Columban Kells was founded for the purpose of refuge, it also appears to have been established with political motives in mind. Had refuge been the sole concern of the Columban *familia* they could surely have settled in the existing Columban monastery of Durrow, which had attracted the support of Clann Cholmáin kings of Tara during the previous century.[35] Máire Herbert has suggested that Clann Cholmáin's political aims were the motivation for the new foundation: 'Clann Cholmáin may have favoured the transfer of the site of Kells to the Columban *familia* for reasons which may have been more pragmatic than altruistic, being concerned with weakening the influence in the area of their Síl nÁedo Sláine rivals'.[36] Kells, however, was constructed during the reign of a Cenél nEógain king of Tara, Áed Oirdnide (*ob*.819), and not a Clann Cholmáin king. F.J. Byrne suggested that even so, political motivations may still have influenced any royal grant of land to the Columban *familia* for the foundation. Áed Oirdnide's uncle and also king of Tara, Áed Allán, had been killed by Murchad Midi, the first Clann Cholmáin king of Tara, at Seredmag near Kells.[37] Therefore Áed Oirdnide may have sought to grant away a site associated with Clann Cholmáin's rise to power and which may, therefore, have held some prestige in their eyes.[38] Neither theory is without its flaws. The evidence for Clann Cholmáin involvement is, as Herbert admits, speculative.[39] It is also unclear why Áed Oirdnide of Cenél nEógain would support the granting of Kells to the Columban *familia*, which was linked to both his Southern Uí Néill rivals (Clann Cholmáin) and Northern Uí Néill rivals (Cenél Conaill).

Although the circumstances are now impossible to uncover, it is reasonable to assume that – as so often the case in the medieval period – pietistic and political motives both played their parts.[40]

Kells grew into a centre of great wealth during the first millennium, as witnessed by the erection of high-crosses and construction of a round tower, and Charles Doherty has argued that the Book of Kells itself may have been commissioned for the dedication of a new church at Kells in 814 (although Iona remains a strong contender for its site of production).[41] The vernacular *Betha Adamnáin* ('Life of Adomnán'), a hagiography celebrating the former abbot of Iona (*ob.*704), was also probably composed at Kells in the middle of the 10th century.[42] Such wealth naturally attracts attention, and the settlement was plundered in 920.[43] One of the most spectacular raids by Dublin Vikings on Kells and other midland churches occurred in 951 and resulted in three thousand captives taken, along with cattle, horses, gold and silver.[44] The plunder taken in subsequent raids in 970, 997 and 1019 are a testimony to the vitality of the settlement and economy of Kells.[45]

Even before these raids, Kells was already embroiled in the violent internal politics of Clann Cholmáin, when it may have been the base (perhaps unwillingly) for a revolt against the high king, Flann Sinna, in 904.[46] By the beginning of the 11th century Kells appears to have been acknowledged as the seat of the *comarba* ('heir') of Colum Cille and became closely bound to Clann Cholmáin kings of Mide.[47] This link is clearly expressed in a warning to the Clann Cholmáin king of Mide/Tara, Conchobor ua Maíl Shechnaill (*ob.*1073), in his 11th-century *notitia* recording a grant to the church of Kildalkey: 'and though it is risky for anyone to flout Colum Cille, it is more risky for a king, and though it is risky for any king, it is more risky for the king of Tara, for he is kin to Colum Cille'.[48]

The *notitiae* in the Book of Kells, Herbert claims, characterize Kells of this period as a 'property-conscious, proto-urban centre'.[49] Bairbre Nic Aongusa has argued that the considerable degree of buying and selling, mention of a market (*margad*) and the recording of inflation in the *notitiae* all suggest that Kells may be termed a market town.[50] Mary Valante subsequently argued against the validity of the idea of a monastic town,[51] while Colmán Etchingham has likewise poured scorn on the concept.[52] Regardless of whether Kells may be classified as a town, monastic town, urban or proto-urban centre, it seems clear that the Kells region was an enduring centre of wealth. Consequently, the 11th- and 12th-century *notitiae*, which reflect this, prove an interesting point of departure for an analysis of the methods used by competing kings to control this valuable area, not least Tigernán Ua Ruairc.

3. The royal grants in the Book of Kells

Tigernán Ua Ruairc's grant of Mag nDechrad to Kells is recorded among a very small but highly informative group of documents known as *notitiae* (notes of land transactions), which survive in the great Gaelic gospel books of the early medieval period. Their scarcity was highlighted by Gearóid Mac Niocaill (the greatest scholar of this material), who noted *níl ach fíorbheagán samplaí de cháipéisí Gaeilge ar marthain ón dtréimhse réamhNormannach: 12 cheann as Leabhar Cheanannais ... ceann amháin i Leabhar Dhurmhagh ... agus 5 cinn (as Albain) i Leabhar Dhéir* ('There are very few samples of [administrative] documents in Irish surviving from the pre-Norman period: twelve from the Book of Kells ... one in the Book of Durrow ... and five (from Scotland) in the Book of Deer').[1] The value of these administrative documents for the study of royal power and how a king like Tigernán Ua Ruairc acted on the ground is seen in their portrayal of land transactions; a portrayal that contrasts markedly with other classes of sources, such as hagiography. Documents like *notitiae* and charters, while not without their own caprices (for example, the occasional provision of flattering titles), often provide a great deal of contemporary information, such as witness lists and chronological material concerning the date of the transactions recorded in them. This information also provides grounds for commentary on the political and social environment in which the transactions occurred and were recorded. In contrast, in hagiographic accounts of land grants the writers often deliberately obscured the details of contemporary land transactions. Hagiographers almost invariably portrayed gifts of land as actions that took place during the lifetimes of the subject of the work and an important ancestor of the contemporary donor. This convention impedes the study of some contemporary aspects of transactions recorded by hagiographers, for example, the identification of minor secular lords who may have had an interest in individual transactions. The latter are much easier to identify from other sources, such as *notitiae* guarantor lists (lists of those who vowed to ensure the implementation of an agreement's terms). A good example of this may be seen by contrasting the Mag nDechrad *notitia* (which contains reliable details of a 12th-century land transfer from Ua Ruairc to Kells), with a contemporary hagiographic text, the Middle Irish Life of Colum Cille, which seeks to anchor Kells' founding in Columba's time and obscures its 9th-century context.

ADMINISTRATIVE DOCUMENTS AND RELIGIOUS MANUSCRIPTS

The illuminated gospel books (i.e., those highly decorated in colour) that contain the surviving *notitiae* in their margins and blank leaves were all originally written a number of centuries prior to the recording of the notes. Administrative record-keeping of this kind is also found in manuscripts from Anglo-Saxon England and Wales, where earlier gospel books and other religious manuscripts contain a variety of memoranda that were written into them between the 9th and 12th centuries.[2] Furthermore, in Scotland, records from Loch Leven survive in a cartulary (register of charters) of the Augustinian priory of St Andrews, which acquired Loch Leven in the middle of the 12th century. These Latin records appear to have been written originally in Gaelic, and it is possible (though unprovable) that they were initially written in a Gospel Book.[3] In the Gaelic-speaking world three gospel books – the Book of Kells, the Book of Durrow and the Book of Deer – contain records of land transactions.[4] All three are associated with churches that venerated St Columba, contain a number of illuminations (although those of Deer are far cruder than the other two) and the gospel books of Kells and Durrow may even have been considered relics of Columba.[5]

With regard to the use of a gospel book as a repository for administrative documents, the earliest editor and translator of the Kells *notitiae*, John O'Donovan, suggested that the *notitiae* were 'probably transcribed from the original deeds into this sacred and venerable book in order to secure their preservation'.[6] O'Donovan's view that these documents were charters may have led him to assume that they were originally issued on individual diplomata and only later assembled in the manuscript, like a monastic cartulary. However, it seems likely that all but one of the *notitiae* were contemporary entries in the Book of Kells,[7] yet he is doubtless correct that the authors looked upon the great manuscript as a means of protecting them. Indeed entering them into gospel books may have added an extra layer of solemnity and inviolability to them. David Dumville has even gone so far as to claim, with respect to the status of Anglo-Saxon transaction records in religious manuscripts, that they 'became in some measure *liturgica* themselves'.[8]

Such measures were not foolproof, and although gospel book records seem to have had a greater chance of survival than isolated diplomata, the records contained within them were not immutable. For example, the Deer *notitiae* show signs of deletion and reworking and Anglo-Saxon manuscripts display similar processes.[9] This was not simply a case of revising and updating older material but rather, in some cases, a deliberate expurgation of the record. As Dumville has noted, with regard to the Anglo-Saxon evidence, there are 'suspicious excision of leaves, half leaves, or marginal strips from gospel-books in particular', which suggest that other administrative records may have existed.[10] Accidents of transmission and deliberate censorship of records may account for the loss of some Gaelic *notitiae*. Be this as it may, it appears somewhat coincidental that the few surviving Gaelic *notitiae* are all found in manuscripts emanating from Columban monasteries, and it must be asked whether the *notitiae*, at least in a Gaelic environment, were a Columban phenomenon.

THE *NOTITIAE*: A COLUMBAN TRADITION?

The majority of the surviving records concerning Deer relate to a Cistercian monastery founded at Deer (Aberdeenshire, north-east Scotland) in 1219 by the earl of Buchan, William Comyn, and the earliest account of a pre-Cistercian monastery at Deer is that located in the Book of Deer itself.[11] In that manuscript six Gaelic *notitiae* mention Columba as a recipient of grants made. The first *notitia* is essentially a hagiographic foundation legend involving Columba, which may have been invented at the time of the writing of the Deer *notitiae*.[12] In contrast, the establishment of the monasteries of Durrow and Kells are better recorded. Columba founded Durrow, according to the testimony of early commentators such as Adomnán (*ob.*704),[13] and it seems to have had a position of prominence among the Columban *familia* during its early existence, while continuing to be important between the 8th and 11th centuries.[14] In the early 12th century, when the lone Book of Durrow *notitia* was written, Gilla Adomnáin, the priest of that church, subsequently became the abbot of Kells, following the murder of the previous abbot.[15] Although this may have been an expedient arrangement, it nonetheless signifies that Durrow was close to the centre of Columban affairs at the time the Durrow *notitia* was written. Lastly, Kells is the only church of the three whose foundation can be dated with reasonable certainty. Its establishment in 807 was recorded in the contemporary Annals of Ulster, and Kells even succeeded in becoming the premier church of the *familia* of Columba by the beginning of the 11th century,[16] and was the seat of the *comarba* of Columba during the period to which a number of the Kells *notitiae* refer.

Richard Sharpe has suggested it is possible that the existence of *notitiae* in the three gospel books indicate a short-lived Columban revival of a form of document derived from the British-Latin charter.[17] While it is tempting to see the two sets of notes in the Books of Kells and Deer, along with the lone note in the Book of Durrow, as part of a common method of recording land transactions among the Columban community, the Columban link should not be overstated. The nature and even existence of a Columban community at this time (in the sense of a network of churches in a close and formal relationship) is far from certain. As Herbert pointed out, 'by the twelfth century the horizons of the successors of Colum Cille in Kells seemed to be contracting to the immediate – and largely secularized – concerns of their own monastery'.[18] Indeed, Deer may not necessarily have been part of the Columban *familia* at all; although it may have been dedicated to Columba (and St Drostan) this need not indicate a formal relationship with other similarly dedicated churches. As circumstantial proof of its external position, it may be noted that although Kells and Durrow appear to have occasionally shared ecclesiastical personnel (such as Gilla Adomnáin), there are no records of similar links between these churches and Deer. Differences also exist within their *notitiae*, and although there are a number of similarities between the land transaction documents found in all three gospel books, Dauvit Broun has demonstrated that the Kells and Deer *notitiae* not only collectively differ from each other but also display noticeable internal differences.[19] Thus it is unadvisable to attempt to extrapolate a pattern from, or to enforce a uniform interpretation upon, these *notitiae*. The *notitiae*, while valuable for the study of a number of aspects of Gaelic Scotland and Ireland during the 11th and 12th centuries, are nonetheless products of their own individual social, ecclesiastical and political milieu.

THE MANUSCRIPTS AND EDITIONS OF THE KELLS *NOTITIAE*

The Kells dossier amounts to 12 *notitiae*, which are found in six manuscripts, and crucially the Mag nDechrad *notitia* no longer survives in the Book of Kells (owing to loss of leaves from the manuscript) but in 17th- and 18th-century transcripts. The manuscripts across which the *notitiae* are spread are: Trinity College Dublin, 58 (formerly A. 1. 6, known as the Book of Kells); Trinity College Dublin, 580 (formerly E. 3. 8); British Library, Add. 4791; British Library, Egerton 104; Royal Irish Academy, A v 3 and National Library of Ireland, G 583.

Trinity College Dublin 58 is the famous illuminated gospel book known as the Book of Kells and the ultimate ancestor of all the other manuscript copies of these *notitiae*, although owing to the loss of some of its leaves, it now contains only *notitiae* §§1–7. Trinity College Dublin 580 was a copy made from the Book of Kells for Archbishop James Ussher sometime after 1621, and it contains §§1–6, in the same order as the Book of Kells.[20] British Library Add. 4791 is a composite manuscript, that belonged to the antiquarian Sir James Ware, and was made before 1648. It is the only manuscript to contain all 12 *notitiae* (including the Mag nDechrad *notitia*), but as Mac Niocaill noted when editing it:

> It was executed in a secretary hand by a scribe who had just sufficient acquaintance with the Irish script to confuse similar letters; thus, for example: *s f* and *r, c t d o* and *e, h b* and *li*, are frequently confused. Suspension marks are commonly omitted, and almost every error possible has been committed. Nevertheless, it is possible to recognize substantial stretches of Irish, and by comparison with what still survives in the Book of Kells to work out the greater part of what lies behind the transcript.[21]

British Library Egerton 104 contains a 19th-century copy and translation of §6 from the Book of Kells and has no independent value.[22] Similarly National Library of Ireland G 583 is a 19th-century copy of the *notitiae* currently extant in the Book of Kells.[23] The final manuscript, Royal Irish Academy A v 3, was written by the antiquarian Charles O'Conor the elder between 1776 and 1786, and contains a copy of §8 (divided into i and ii), which only otherwise exists (in corrupted form) in Ware's transcript.[24] This latter is the *notitia* that contains Tigernán Ua Ruairc's grant to Int Ednén (§8(i)) and of Mag nDechrad to Kells (§8(ii)). The process by which each transcript came into being is unclear, and since O'Conor's 18th-century copy of §8 is far superior to Ware's it cannot have derived from it, but likewise it is highly unlikely to have been copied directly from the Book of Kells. Consequently Mac Niocaill suggested that O'Conor's transcript was made from an intermediary copy, which may have derived directly from the Book of Kells itself.[25]

The *notitiae* have been edited four times and translated three times.[26] In the 19th century, John O'Donovan – who was only aware of the existence of the Book of Kells and Ussher's transcript – edited and translated only *notitiae* §§1–7. Mac Niocaill knew of the existence of all the manuscripts (except National Library of Ireland G 583) and made use of all the manuscripts known to him (except British Library Egerton 104) for his 1961 edition, *Notitiae as Leabhar Cheanannais*. He utilized the same manuscripts for his 1990 re-edition and translation, 'The Irish "Charters"', admitting that his previous edition contained 'some rash restorations'.[27]

SCHOLARS AND THE *NOTITIAE*

The study of these *notitiae* has mainly centred on whether or not an administrative documentary tradition existed in pre-Norman Ireland, the legal status of the *notitiae* and whether they can be considered charters or some form of proto-charter. Their earliest editor and translator, John O'Donovan, seems to have had little doubt that they were charters, hence the title of his 1846 edition 'The Irish charters in the Book of Kells'. He pronounced, with a certain national pride, that 'these Charters are exceedingly interesting to the historian, as proving that the ancient Irish had committed their covenants to writing in their own language before the Anglo-Norman invasion'.[28] O'Donovan continued by directly equating them with 'the other extant Charters made in Ireland at the same period', which 'are all in the Latin language'.[29] Only five charters survive from the pre-invasion period, all of which were issued to reformers or continental monastic orders that had recently arrived in Ireland (one by the high-king Muirchertach Mac Lochlainn and four by Diarmait Mac Murchada, king of Laigin).[30] O'Donovan also linked the *notitiae* with entries in the early 9th-century Book of Armagh, presumably the *Additamenta* (additional material) to

Tírechán's account of St Patrick's itinerary.[31] His analysis ended with a comment that contained the seeds of much future discussion: 'it is more than probable that hundreds of such deeds were preserved in the Irish monasteries, but it must be confessed that very few of them are now known to our antiquarians, if indeed they have survived the ravages of time'.[32]

James Kenney, in a magisterial survey of written sources from medieval Ireland published in 1929, suggested that surviving administrative documentary sources, such as *notitiae*, are scarce because they never existed in appreciable quantities.[33] In contrast, Mac Niocaill broadly agreed with O'Donovan and suggested that *is deáratach, d'ainneoin a laghaid atá againn, go mbídís cuíosach coitianta tráth. Is léir go raibh taithí éigin in Éirinn ar fhianaise cháipéiseach anuas ó thúas an 8ú céid* ('it is possible, despite the small number of them we have, that they were once reasonably common. It is clear that there was some experience in Ireland of administrative documents from the beginning of the 8th century onwards').[34] In support of his theory Mac Niocaill drew on a number of sources, but acknowledged that there is a major gap in the record of this supposed tradition, between the 8th and 11th centuries.[35] Mac Niocaill dubbed the records in the Kells dossier *notitiae*, claiming that they were 'notes akin to an *aide-mémoire*, not having the same evidential value as a formal charter'.[36] A factor that may have influenced the adoption of this terminology was his belief that these memoranda, which he thought were all recorded in the Book of Kells during the third quarter of the 12th century, were compiled in order to obtain a charter confirming Kells' possessions from the new English lord of Meath, Hugh de Lacy (*ob.*1186).[37]

In the early 1980s, in a volume dedicated to Kathleen Hughes, Wendy Davies proposed the existence of a 'Celtic Charter'.[38] This type of charter, Davies claimed, was characterized by two main features, namely the use of the past tense (which indicates that these 'charters' were evidential rather than dispositive i.e. they provided evidence for a previous grant rather than being the instrument of the grant itself), and a tripartite structure consisting of a disposition (particulars relating to what was given), a witness list and a sanction clause (pronouncing maledictions on those who would transgress the terms of the agreement). According to these criteria, *notitiae* §§1–4 are the only 'Celtic Charters' in the Kells dossier.[39] However, as Hughes asked in her seminal study of the 'Celtic church', it must also be asked of the 'Celtic Charter' – 'is this a valid concept?'.[40] Davies' model has been the subject of some searing criticism, most notably by Dauvit Broun.[41]

Further cogent surveys of the Irish administrative documentary tradition include those of Máire Herbert[42] and Marie Therese Flanagan.[43] Herbert's summary highlights issues of transmission and she has suggested that many early legal records may have been destroyed as a result of Viking activity and that others may have been discarded as they were no longer relevant in later medieval Ireland.[44] Flanagan, in her edition and translation of Latin charters issued by

Irish kings during the 12th and 13th centuries, provided the most comprehensive discussion of non-literary administrative documentation in pre-Norman Ireland to date, and argued that the *notitiae* may be broadly seen as part of a 'Celtic Charter' tradition, but that Davies' criteria are somewhat restrictive.[45]

This scholarship on the *notitiae* has focused on their position within the Irish documentary tradition and their status as legal documents,[46] and aside from Mac Niocaill, the only detailed discussions of the contents of the texts are those of Bairbre Nic Aongusa,[47] Máire Herbert,[48] and the present author.[49] In her studies, Nic Aongusa used the *notitiae* as the basis for investigating the hierarchy of the community of Kells and an exploration of two economic issues: the extent of Kells' monastic holdings and the extent of trade in the 'monastic town' of Kells.[50] Herbert's article, 'Charter material from Kells', sought not only to assess the status of the *notitiae* but also the insights they offered into 'the practice of property transfers, and into the social, political, economic, and ecclesiastical worlds in which they are situated'.[51] In something of a development on this latter approach, the next chapter seeks to use Tigernán's Mag nDechrad *notitia* as evidence for the political and social environment in which the grant occurred and was recorded, and in doing so, will attempt to illuminate the history of the greater Kells area and Bréifne during the middle of the 12th century.

4. Tigernán Ua Ruairc's grant of Mag nDechrad to Kells

Short though it is, much more may be gleaned from the *notitia* recording Tigernán Ua Ruairc's grant of Mag nDechrad to Kells than simply evidence for issues of documentary form. The Mag nDechrad *notitia* provides information on the extent of Bréifne in the middle of the 12th century (which can be obtained by analyzing the title afforded Tigernán and the significance of the named boundary points of his kingdom) and on the extent of the lands granted (also discernable through placename analysis). In turn, this provides grounds for suggesting a date for the grant (*c.*1152), and exploring the identities and interests of those Bréifne grandees who stood as guarantors for it. This sheds light on the greater Kells area, the motivations (both pious and political) for granting land to the church of Kells, and the extent of the sway and ambition of the man who would be king over it all.

THE TEXT

The Mag nDechrad *notitia* reads in full:

> *Ro edhbair dano in Tighernan cetna .i. ardri Airthir Connacht et na Telach archena o Thrácht Eothaile co Magh Tlachtgha et o Shinaind co Drochat Atha Magh nDechrad uile o Ath O Chan[n]anán co cend in Rois et o Rind i[n] Daire co Domhnach Mór .i. ferond cen mess [cen] chlais i mbithdhilsi do Dhía et do Cholum Cille úadh féin et [o] cech rígh gébhas Brefne co bráth a comhairle maithe fer mBrefne eter Ua Briúin et Conmhaicne co ndola doibh féin i slanaighecht na hedhbarta. Et itét so na slána .i. Gaphraidh Ua Raghallaigh et Lorcán Ua Donnchadha o Mhuintir Maelmórdha et Gilla Padraic mac meic Fiachrach o Chlaind Chathail et Imar mac Tighernán o Chenél Brénaind et Gilla Cíaran Ua Draighnén comharba Fechén.*

The same Tigernán also gave i.e. overking of East Connacht and of the Telacha in addition from Trácht Eothaile to Mag Tlachtga and from the Shannon to Droichet Átha all Mag nDechrad from Áth Uí Chanannáin to the end of the Ros and from Rind in Daire to Domnach Mór i.e. land without wood or tillage as a perpetual alienation to God and to Colum Cille from himself and from every king that shall take Bréifne for ever,

by the counsel of the nobles of the men of Bréifne both Uí Briúin and
Conmaicne, and they themselves went as guarantors for the gift. And
these are the guarantors: Gofraid Ua Ragallaig and Lorcán Ua Donnchada
from Muintir Maíl Mórda and Gilla Pátraic grandson of Fiachra from
Clann Chathail and Ímar son of Tigernán from Cenél Brénainn and Gilla
Ciaráin Ua Draignén successor of Féchín.[1]

The words *in Tighernan cetna* ('the same Tigernán') in the opening sentence
suggest that this record was intended to be read in conjunction with that of
the previous grant, which was a donation by Tigernán to Int Ednén, while
dano ('also/moreover') further links the two *notitiae* (which may explain why
Tigernán was not afforded a title in the initial Int Ednén *notitia*).[2] The use of *in
Tighernan cetna* and *dano* also suggests that the ordering of these two *notitiae*, as
they now stand, is the same as that found in their exemplar(s). Consequently
it seems strange that Tigernán's title should be registered in the second *notitia*
and not the first, but a possible explanation is that the title recorded may have
been a marginal or interlinear gloss which was subsequently incorporated into
the text, as it now survives. There are two reasons for believing that this may
have been so. First, Tigernán's title is prefaced with the explanatory markers *.i.*
in Royal Irish Academy A v 3 (O'Conor's transcript) and *ygon* (*edón*) in British
Library Add. 4791 (Ware's transcript). Second, Droichet Átha (Drogheda) (the
last named of the four extremities of Tigernán's domain) appears directly before
Mag nDechrad (the land granted), which results in the grant reading rather
clumsily. If Tigernán's title and domain description (*.i. ardri Airthir Connacht et
na Telach archena o Thrácht Eothaile co Magh Tlachtgha et o Shinaind co Drochat Atha*)
were removed, then the resulting opening would be much clearer: *Ro edhbair
dano in Tighernan cetna Magh nDechrad uile o* ... ('The same Tigernán also gave
all Mag nDechrad from ... '). Mac Niocaill offered good reasons for believing
that neither Ware's nor O'Conor's copy of this *notitia* was made directly from
the Book of Kells, but since this possible gloss is substantially similar in both
it stands to reason that both manuscripts drew on an earlier copy in which
the gloss had already been incorporated.[3] Nonetheless, even if Tigernán's title
and the boundary points enumerated were a gloss, it is quite possible that they
were a gloss on the original *notitia* in the Book of Kells, and were roughly
contemporary with the recording of the *notitia* and possibly even the grant itself.

TIGERNÁN'S TITLE AND KINGDOM

The term *ardri Airthir Connacht* ('overking/highking of east Connacht') is a title
associated exclusively with Uí Briúin Bréifne (who were primarily located
east of the Shannon), as only members of Uí Ruairc were called kings of east
Connacht in the annals (and mainly only in the 11th century too). The first

use of the term *rí Airthir Connacht* dates from 1039: *Doncadh Derg mac Airt Uallaigh h-Úi Ruairc, rígdamna Brefne, do marbadh la h-Aedh h-Úa Concobair (.i. Aed in Ga Bernaig) fria lamaib a athar, ocus ba ri Airrtir Condacht uile in Dondcadhsin* ('Donnchad the Red, son of Art Uallach Ua Ruairc, *rígdomna* of Bréifne, was killed by Áed Ua Conchobair (that is, Áed of the Gapped-Spear), instead of his father; and that Donnchad was king of the whole of east Connacht').[4] Donnchad's father, Art, was later described as king of Connacht on his death in 1046,[5] which suggests that Donnchad's position, as king of east Connacht (and certainly as *rígdamna Bréifne*), was a subordinate one. In the year after Art's death, his son Níall, *rí Brefne ocus Airrthir Connacht*, was also killed.[6] Another son of Art, Áed Ua Ruairc, killed a Cathal Ua Ruairc (*rí Brefne ocus Airrthir Chondacht*) in an internecine struggle in 1059.[7] In the 1084 obit of Donnchad mac Airt (*in Cailech*, 'the Cock'), who appears in one Kells *notitia* under the somewhat flattering title of rí Connacht ocus Galeng ('king of Connacht and Gailenga'), Donnchad is called both *rí Breifne* and *rí Airthir Connacht*.[8] The title 'king of east Connacht' does not appear in the annals again for almost 40 years, until the death of Tigernán's father, Áed,[9] and later again is found in the Life of the Connacht saint, Berach. In that Life, Berach is said to have transformed Áed Dub, an ugly king of Bréifne and ancestor of Uí Ruairc, into a handsome man, which resulted in Áed receiving the byname Finn, in place of Dub: *conadh desin ainmnigter sliocht Aodha finn o ttad riogradh oirthir Connacht* ('so it is from this is named the Slicht Áeda Finn (progeny of Áed Finn), from whom are [descended] the royal line of east Connacht').[10]

It is possible that the title *rí Airthir Connacht* reflects attempts by the Uí Ruairc to expand into east Connacht, particularly into Mag Lurg and Mag nAí in modern Co. Roscommon. In 1095, while the high-king Muirchertach Ua Briain was engaged in an extensive campaign in the midlands, the Annals of Inisfallen report: *Foslongphort hic Muirchertach hi Maig Hoa Fiacrach o medon samaraid co Feil Michil coro inarbait les Sil Muirethaig ocus Conmacne a Maig Aí ocus a Maig Luirg isin DubBréfne sís* ('Muirchertach had an encampment in Mag Ua Fiachrach from mid-summer until the Feast of Michael, and he banished Síl Muiredaig and the Conmaicne from Mag nAí and Mag Lurg downwards into Black Bréifne').[11] Similarly, in the decade prior to Tigernán's accession to the kingship of Uí Briúin Bréifne, Tairdelbach Ua Conchobair, king of Connacht, also banished the Conmaicne from Mag nAí (in 1114), perhaps implying that they had returned and were again unwelcome.[12] In the 11th and 12th centuries the term Conmaicne was most commonly used for Conmaicne Réin (a people located in the modern counties of Leitrim and Longford), who were vassals of Uí Briúin Bréifne.[13] Indeed, so closely were they linked that Áed Ua Ruairc, king of Uí Briúin Bréifne at the time of the 1114 expulsion and called *rí Airthir Connacht* by the Annals of Tigernach and Chronicon Scotorum, was entitled *rí Conmaicne* ('king of Conmaicne') by other annalistic compilations upon his death.[14] Subsequently, in the 12th century, the Conmaicne Réin expanded southwards into Tethba (Co. Longford) under Uí Ruairc and founded the new lordships of Muintir Eólais (ruled by Mac Ragnaill) and Muintir Angaile (ruled by Uí Fhergail).[15] It is possible that Uí Ruairc may have been using their Conmaicne vassals to colonize land west of the Shannon no later than the late 11th/early 12th centuries, if not earlier.[16] Consequently, the title *rí Airthir Connacht* may have been adopted to celebrate and promote Uí Briúin Bréifne expansion, both through the use of Conmaicne vassals and their own acquisition of land in modern Co. Sligo.[17]

Although the annalistic evidence suggests that Airthir Connacht and Bréifne were separate entities, Tigernán's title in the *notitia* (*ardri Airthir Connacht et na Telach archena*) suggests that Bréifne was located in either Airthir Connacht or *na Telacha*. However, the title *rí Airthir Connacht* may not have been a static appellation. The repeated (or indeed fitful) use of a title over a period does not mean that it held the same force during that entire time. Just as the kingdom of Bréifne (and other kingdoms, such as Mide) differed greatly in extent between the mid-11th and mid-12th centuries, the continued use of titles, such as *rí Bréifne* (or *rí Mide*), conceal those political changes. Indeed, *rí Airthir Connacht*, may not primarily have had a territorial context in each instance of its use, but may originally have been reflective of Uí Ruairc ambitions towards obtaining the kingship of all Connacht during the 11th century. By claiming the kingship of Connacht (or part thereof), Uí Ruairc may have been stressing their membership of the Connachta and advertising that they were of 'provincial king' status.

Mac Niocaill suggested that the second part of Tigernán's title, *airdri ... na Telach archena* ('overking/highking ... of the Tellacha in general'), refers to Tellach nDúnchadha and Tellach nEchach (baronies of Tullyhunco and Tullyhaw, Co. Cavan, respectively).[18] These were probably the earliest homelands of the Uí Briúin,[19] and Tellach Gairbheth and Tellach Cerbaill (baronies of Tullygarvey and Upper Loughtee, Co. Cavan, respectively) may probably be added to this list as well. It is unclear what the force of *archena* is in this sentence. It may be taken to mean that *na Telacha* were not understood as part of *Airthir Connacht* and that *archena* should be translated as 'besides' or 'in addition'. Alternatively, though perhaps less likely, *archena* may mean 'in general', suggesting that *Airthir Connacht* was intended to mean a constituent part of *na Telacha*. The inclusion of *na Telacha* may not have simply been a statement of territorial lordship. It may have been an expression of Tigernán's dominion over members of lesser branches of Uí Briúin Bréifne and Conmaicne, a number of which contain the prefix Telach- in their names.[20] It is even possible that *na Telacha* represents Bréifne expansion (or desire to expand) into Southern Uí Néill territory. The kings of Telach Ard (Cenél Lóegaire) and Telach Cail (Delbna) appear as dependents of the Uí Maíl Shechnaill overkings of Mide in other Kells *notitiae*, but the border was moving steadily toward them. Indeed in the 1160s the king of Cenél Lóegaire may have shot himself in the foot by selling back his billeting rights at the church of Ardbraccan, leaving his kingdom increasingly exposed to the threat of annexation by Bréifne.[21]

The four geographical points of Tigernán's kingdom in this grant suggest that his domain had expanded at the expense of a number of minor kingdoms, most notably those previously controlled by the Southern Uí Néill kingdom of Mide (see Fig. 2). These former Uí Néill territories, as Tigernán's title and the four boundary points supplied in this grant suggest, were now considered to be part of *Airthir Connacht* and *na Telacha*. The first boundary point mentioned, Trácht Eothaile (Trawohelly Strand, near Ballysadare, Co. Sligo), not only delineates the north-western extent of Uí Briúin Bréifne expansion but also demonstrates Tigernán's acute strategic sense. Domination of the Sligo coastline and control of the main route between Connacht and the north may have been a factor in the rise of Uí Briúin Bréifne, and their interest in this area stretched back almost a century before Tigernán's reign. In 1029 Áed Ua Ruairc died in a fire in Cairpre (Co. Sligo) along with a substantial number of people, including the *airchinnech* (head of the church) of Druim Cliab (Drumcliff, Co. Sligo), and was entitled king of Cairpre by the Annals of Tigernach.[22] It appears that Uí Ruairc were already expanding into the kingdom of Cairpre Dromma Cliab at this point, while the local Uí Fhlannacáin lords of Cairpre were dispossessed and eventually became the rulers of Fir Manach (Fermanagh).[23] Trácht Eothaile, on the Sligo coastline, was presumably part of the territory acquired during this expansion. Continued Uí Ruairc presence in this area is reflected in the early 12th-century diocesan boundaries. In the 17th century, Geoffrey Keating claimed (citing the earlier, now lost, Book of Clonenagh) that the Synod of Ráith Bressail (1111) had fixed Sraith an Fhearainn (Shramore, near Ballysadare) as one of the boundary points of the north Connacht diocese of Killala.[24] Furthermore, Keating named Ceis Corainn (Keishcorran), approximately 17km south of Ballysadare, as the western point of the adjoining diocese of Ardagh/Ardcarn, which encompassed the territory of Uí Ruairc's subordinates, Conmaicne Réin.[25] The ecclesiastical boundaries doubtlessly reflected the political map of the time and thus it appears that this area of modern Sligo was a region of political and ecclesiastical borders. The extension of the diocese of Ardagh/Ardcarn (i.e., that of Uí Ruairc dependents) to this district suggests that Uí Ruairc maintained an interest in the Sligo region during the early 12th century.

The importance of this area was clearly recognized by Tairdelbach Ua Conchobair, king of Connacht. He erected one of the three castles (*caisdeoil*) that he built in 1124 at Cúl Maíle (Collooney), just south of Ballysadare.[26] While the nature of the construction of these castles is uncertain, the use of this new terminology may be suggestive of innovative building techniques and that these constructions were reasonably substantial. Tairdelbach was an energetic builder and fortified a number of strategic locations in Connacht during his career, such as the Shannon crossing at Athlone, where he also built a castle.[27] The construction at Cúl Maíle was doubtlessly intended by Tairdelbach as a means of protecting the northern entrance to Connacht from Cenél Conaill or Cenél nEógain attacks and also as a staging post for possible expeditions against the north. The modern road network, influenced by pre-existing routes, demonstrates the strategic value of Cúl Maíle to Tairdelbach. Even today Collooney (Cúl Maíle) lies adjacent to the N15 (which is the main route from Connacht to Donegal Town) and stands near the fork of the N17 (the main road towards Co. Galway and ecclesiastical centres such as Tuam) and the N4 (which leads into Co. Roscommon and the early 12th-century Síl Muiredaig heartland of Mag nAí).

As Trácht Eothaile is located a mere 3km north of Cúl Maíle, it suggests that Tigernán also recognized the importance of this route and had an interest in this politically and militarily sensitive area. As he was allied to both the kings of Connacht and Cenél nEógain at various points during his career, it probably made sense to maintain a presence in the area where their domains met. They would thus be more likely to court him in order to carry out their military adventures, for fear he would use his control of this area to thwart their campaigns. The value of Trácht Eothaile for the purpose of this political game was amply demonstrated in the previous century when Brian Bóroma was checked there while attempting to subdue the north of Ireland.[28]

The second geographical point, Mag Tlachtga, presumably refers to the southern extremity of Tigernán's domain. This is almost certainly the area around Tlachtga (the hill of Ward, Co. Meath), approximately 12km south of Kells. This area was located deep within former Southern Uí Néill territory, and significantly, was also associated with the kingship of Tara. A poem ascribed to Cúán ua Lothcháin (*ob.*1024), poet to the last great Southern Uí Néill king of Tara, Máel Sechnaill mac Domnaill, prescribes water from the well of Tlachtga as one of the seven *buada* ('lucky things/victories') of the king of Tara,[29] while Máel Sechnaill won his final battle against the Norse of Dublin at Áth Buide Tlachtga (Athboy, barony of Lune, Co. Meath), a month before he died in 1022.[30] It was at Tlachtga too that Tigernán met his own end in 1172, killed while parleying with the English adventurer Hugh de Lacy.[31] It is likely that Tlachtga was at or near the border of Tigernán's domain and was therefore chosen, as a potentially neutral venue, for the site of that fateful meeting.

The eastern and western boundary markers are given as Droichet Átha and the river Shannon. Diarmuid Ó Murchadha suggested that Droichet Átha (which gives its name to modern Drogheda, Co. Louth) was originally at Oldbridge, Co. Meath.[32] For the purpose of this discussion it matters little, as Drogheda and Oldbridge are only 3km apart and both names imply a bridged crossing of the river Boyne. Droichet Átha spans a vital river crossing and its geographic and strategic importance was very similar to that of Trácht Eothaile. The drumlin belt, which makes the Sligo coastal route the only viable entrance to the north from the west, stretches right across Ireland to the coast of modern Co. Down. The 'topographical chaos' it causes in modern counties Cavan and Monaghan, where it is at its widest,[33] means that a coastal route through modern Co. Louth is the simplest way to enter the north-east of Ireland by land. This is also reflected in the modern road network: the M1 extends from Dublin, through Oldbridge, as far as Dundalk (the edge of the drumlin belt). Any army from the north that wished to proceed into Brega and Mide or to Dublin and thence to Laigin and Munster would first have to reach the river crossing at Droichet Átha. Indeed it was at Droichet Átha that Donnchad Ua Ruairc accepted *tuarastal* ('wages/stipend') from Donn Sléibe, king of Ulaid, and entered into a short-lived alliance with him in 1084.[34] If Tigernán could control Droichet Átha it would have afforded him both the same opportunity for political intrigue as control of Trácht Eothaile did. It would also provide a strategic position from which to defend the territory he had acquired at the expense of the Southern Uí Néill.

Just as in the west Tairdelbach Ua Conchobair realized the importance of Trácht Eothaile, so in the east Tigernán was not the only one to appreciate the value of controlling the area around Droichet Átha. Uí Cherbaill of Airgialla were also expanding rapidly and competing with Uí Ruairc for possession of Southern Uí Néill territory in Brega. In 1125 Muirchertach Ua Cerbaill, king of Airgialla, was killed and his army slaughtered by the men of Mide at Drogheda, which suggests that he may have been attempting to assert Airgialla control in this area,[35] and by 1130 Uí Cherbaill had conquered the Ulaid kingdom of Conaille Muirtheimne (north Louth).[36] In the 1130s the king of Airgialla, Tigernán's half-brother Donnchad Ua Cerbaill, continued the southward expansion of his predecessors from his base in Fernmag (barony of Farney, Co. Monaghan). In 1133 his forces attacked Fine Gall (Fingal, north Co. Dublin) and penetrated as far as Lusk before they fought a battle against the men of Dublin at Findabair na nIngen (Fenor, parish of Donore, Co. Meath), near Droichet Átha.[37] In 1136 Fine Gall was again under pressure from Airgialla, as the *airchinnech* of Swords was killed by the men of Fernmag.[38] At the same time war also broke out between Airgialla and Mide,[39] during which the church of Clonard (Co. Meath) was plundered jointly by Airgialla and Uí Briúin Bréifne.[40]

By 1142 Donnchad Ua Cerbaill's territory had expanded so far south that he was in a position to donate land at Mellifont (less than 9km north-west of Drogheda) for the establishment of the first Irish Cistercian monastery. Brendan Smith has suggested that this had the effect of pushing the ecclesiastical border of the province of Armagh farther south than the limit assigned to it (Sliab Breg) at the Synod of Ráith Bressail (1111).[41] Sliab Breg, however, was the southern tip of the diocese of Armagh but not the ecclesiastical province of Armagh (which contained several dioceses). Since the province of Armagh contained the dioceses of Duleek and Clonard (both Co. Meath), the actual southern border of the ecclesiastical province was further south than Smith implies.[42] Territorial adjustments did take place within the confines of the ecclesiastical province of Armagh, and Donnchad's achievement lay in the creation of the diocese of Airgialla (an expanded version of the diocese of Clogher), which received a sizable portion of the southern territory of the diocese of Armagh and did stretch some 15km south of Sliab Breg, but still within the limits of the province of Armagh as set down at Ráith Bressail. A further indication of the extent of Donnchad's territory was the establishment of an Augustinian house at Termonn Féichín (Termonfeckin, Co. Louth, 12km due east of Mellifont), possibly in the same decade.[43]

Tigernán's claims to suzerainty as far as Droichet Átha represents both the expansion of his own rule into this area and a clear attempt to prevent further Uí Cherbaill annexation of territory, by blocking access to the lands south and west of the river Boyne. Tigernán too had his own ecclesiastical support, as demonstrated in a poem by Gilla Modutu Ua Caisside, which is embedded in the long Irish Life of Máedóc of Ferns. Máedóc was the patron of the churches of Drumlane and Rossinver in Bréifne, which had close relationships with Uí Ruairc, as seen by the inclusion of Máel Brigte Ua Fairchellaig of Drumlane as a guarantor in Tigernán's Int Ednén *notitia*.[44] In Gilla Modutu's poem, tribute was claimed in honour of the *meinistir* ('reliquary') of Máedóc *o Droichet Atha gan faill go Druim Lethan* ('from Drogheda without fail, to Drumlane').[45] Gilla Modutu not only wrote on behalf of the community of Máedóc but also seems to have functioned as a court poet to Tigernán, staking out ecclesiastical and political claims as far as Droichet Átha on behalf of both his masters.[46]

The final geographical marker is the river Shannon, which as the longest river in Ireland acts as a natural geographical and political dividing line. Since the source of the river lay within the confines of Uí Briúin Bréifne (whose territory extended to the north and west of it), the Shannon must be understood in the context of this *notitia* as a general (rather than a localized) western boundary marker. The phrase *o Shinaind co Drochat Átha* ('from Shannon to Droichet Átha') may not simply be an expression of the breadth of Tigernán's domain but also an indication of the extent to which Tigernán's kingdom had now subsumed the territory of the Southern Uí Néill. Variants of a similar phrase, *o Shinaind co muir* ('from Shannon to sea'), appear repeatedly in annals of the 9th, 10th and 12th centuries, in expressions of the dimensions of the lands of the Southern Uí Néill. In the 12th century the phrase appears exclusively, with one exception, in connection with the repeated deposition and installation of Uí Maíl Shechnaill kings of Mide by Tairdelbach Ua Conchobair and Muirchertach Mac Lochlainn.[47] As Droichet Átha was almost on the coast, it seems that the phrase used in the *notitia* was an attempt to appropriate the terminology used to describe Uí Néill possessions, as well as the actual land itself.

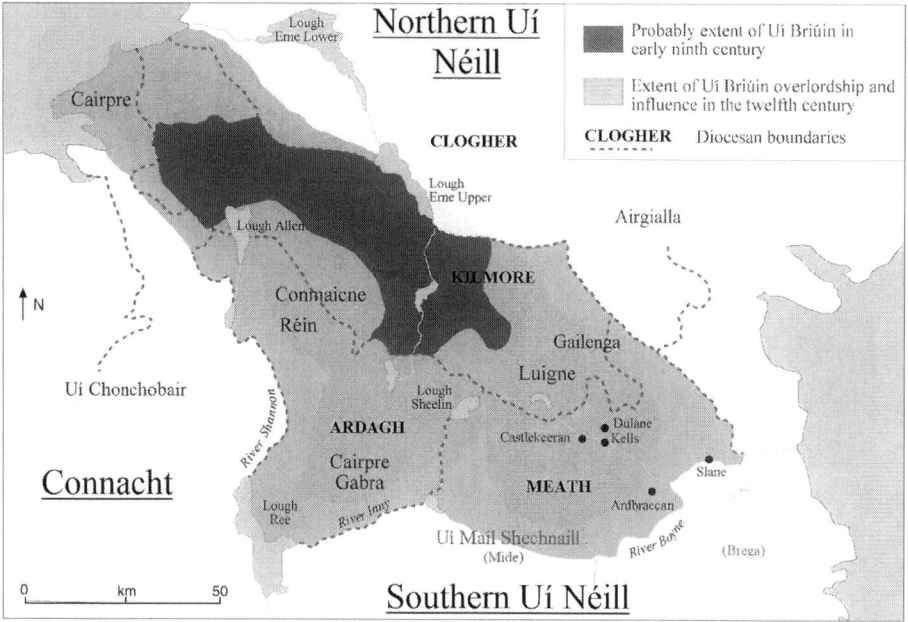

2. Bréifne under Tigernán Ua Ruairc.

THE LANDS GRANTED

Just as Tigernán's domains were delineated by four boundary points in this *notitia*, so too was the land granted, Mag nDechrad ('the plain of Dechrae'). The location and extent of this territory, however, is unclear. In a 14th-century topographical poem by Seaán Mór Ó Dubhagáin, *Triallom timcheall na Fódla*, three *túatha* of Dulane, near Kells, are enumerated. Of these *Fir Eochan do Dheachraidh* ('Fir Eochain are from Dechrae').[48] F.J. Byrne took Dechrae as the nominative singular of the Dechrad of the *notitia* and suggested that Mag nDechrad was in the neighbourhood of Dulane and adjacent to Donaghpatrick, as a Domnach Mór is given as one of the boundary points of the gift in the *notitia*.[49] It has been suggested that Mag nDechrad may be equated with the *Campo Echredd* mentioned in Tírechán's 7th-century Life of Patrick.[50] *Campo Echredd* (rendered Mag nEchredd in Irish) may in turn be identified with the former parish of Moyagher (which is recorded as Moyacherd in the early 14th century),[51] which is now a townland in the parish of Rathmore.[52] In support of the equation of Mag nDechrad with Moyagher, it may be noted that *Haec est charta Moiacher* is written in the margin of the British Library Add. MS 4791 copy of this *notitia* (James Ware's 17th-century copy).[53] If this identification is correct, then Mag nDechrad stretched from Dulane to at least as far as Moyagher, 10km to the south.

Áth Uí Chanannáin, a placename attested nowhere else, may derive its name from the exploits of Ruaidrí Ua Canannáin, king of Cenél Conaill (*ob.*950), who campaigned in the midlands between 947 and 950. In 947 he led an army to Slane (Co. Meath) where he defeated the Norse of Dublin, many of whom drowned.[54] Tomás Ó Canann suggested that Áth Uí Chanannáin ('The Ford of Ua Canannáin') denotes a crossing of the river Boyne at Slane, which he believes was named after Ruaidrí.[55] If this is so, Áth Uí Chanannáin would have been located approximately 20km east-north-east of the townland of Moyagher.

It is not possible to suggest plausible identities for *cend in Rois* ('end of the Ros') and *Rind i[n] Daire* (Rinn in Daire). Nollaig Ó Muraíle has suggested that *cend in Rois* may have given its name to Carnaross in the parish of Loughan/Castlekeeran, 6km north-west of Kells. Carnaross, however, was first attested in 1812.[56] Furthermore, the elements *cend* ('end/head') and *carn* ('heap/mound') have quite different topographical meanings. It is most likely that *cend in Rois*, as Mac Niocaill has translated, is not a placename but a literal description of the boundary point in question, namely the edge of a wooded point. Since the land granted was *cen mess* ('without wood') it is possible that the edge of a wooded area would form a boundary point.

F.J. Byrne considered that the final point, Domnach Mór, was modern Donaghpatrick, the site of an important Patrician church.[57] Ó Canann, however, suggests that Domnach Mór is actually Donaghmore, outside Navan. Although Domnach Pátraic was sometimes referred to as Domnach Mór Pátraic, it is likely, as Ó Canann claims, that had the writer of the *notitia* meant Domnach Pátraic he would have included the saint's name.[58] As the wording of the *notitia* stands, Donaghmore near Navan must be the first choice.

If the above identifications are accepted, then the land Tigernán granted encompassed Dulane in the north, Moyagher in the south, and both Donaghmore and Slane in the east. It is not clear why two eastern boundary points were utilized, although it may not have been considered necessary to specify four locations corresponding to the four cardinal points of the compass. For example, the river Shannon was used as a boundary point of Tigernán's kingdom in this *notitia*, yet due to its length it does not indicate a precise location in the same way as the remaining boundary points do, such as Trácht Eothaile. Likewise, the boundary points of some of the bishoprics created at Ráith Bressail in 1111 did not correspond to the cardinal points, for example Cell dá Lua (Killaloe).[59] In another Kells *notitia*, which dates from the late 11th century, four individuals are named among a long list of guarantors as *cethror comothech assin cetharaird* ('four neighbours from the four points').[60] Even in this instance *cetharaird* does not necessarily mean the four compass points, but in a legal context can simply mean the four nearest neighbours.[61] In the Mag nDechrad

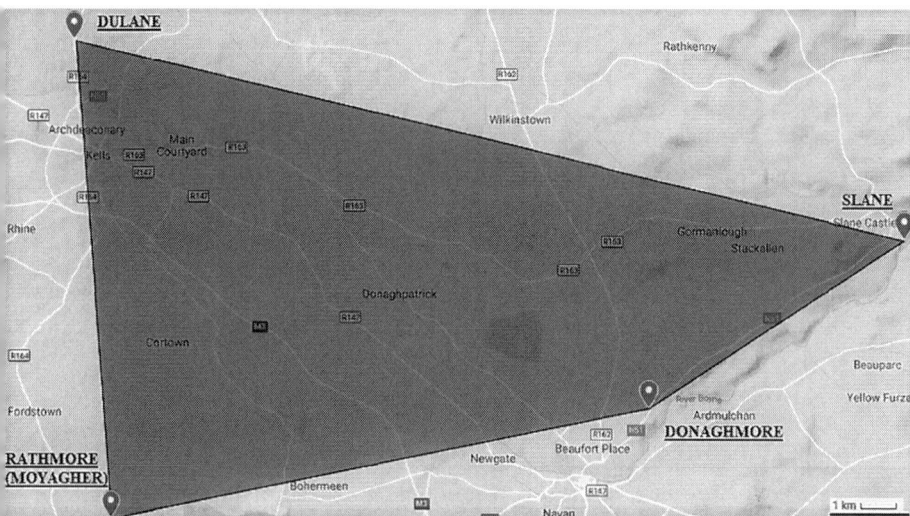

3. Reconstruction of Mag nDechrad as granted by Tigernán Ua Ruairc to Kells.

notitia Donaghmore and Slane may simply have been utilized as boundary points because they were both located on the river Boyne and thus the length of the river between these two points was the intended boundary of the lands granted.

The expanse of land donated by Tigernán was substantial. It comprised of a quadrilateral that measures 10km between Dulane and Moyagher, 12½km between Moyagher and Donaghmore, almost 10km between Donaghmore and Slane and an impressive 23km between Slane and Dulane. Moyagher is only 7½km from Tlachtga and Slane is 12km from Drogheda (9½km from Oldbridge), the southern and eastern boundary points given in Tigernán's title (see Fig. 3). Consequently the land granted was close to the southern and eastern frontiers of Tigernán's kingdom. Interestingly, the territory given by Tigernán encompassed Tailtiu, the site of *Óenach Tailten*. Although this assembly seems to have fallen into disuse among the Uí Néill, the site was important to Uí Néill ideology and Tigernán's grant of this land to the church of Kells may have been intended to deprive his enemies of an area of ideological importance. More recently Tairdelbach Ua Conchobair had celebrated *Óenach Tailten* in 1120, perhaps in an attempt to emphasize the impotency of Uí Maíl Shechnaill, whose king he had banished that year.[62] Thus Tigernán's grant may have been directed against both local Uí Maíl Shechnaill kings and ambitious external rulers such as Ua Conchobair. If Tigernán was motivated by an intention to deny opponents the use of ideologically important sites, then his gift may be viewed as somewhat akin to the high-king Muirchertach Ua Briain's gift of Cashel to the church in 1101, which denied the rival Eóganacht of Munster their key symbolic centre.[63]

The extent and location of the lands granted may be related to the broader political and ecclesiastical events at the possible time of donation. Mac Niocaill suggested that the grant dates between 1137 and 1161.[64] He based these dates upon the career of Gilla Ciaráin Ua Draignén of Fore, *comarba Fechén* ('successor of Féchín'), who is mentioned at the end of the *notitia*. Gilla Ciaráin died in 1161 and had probably held office since the death of a previous *comarba*, Mac Gilla Fhionáin Ua Ciblecháin, in 1137.[65] A more precise date is given in the 18th-century Royal Irish Academy copy of the *notitia*, which is entitled *Charta Tigernani Ó Ruarc AD 1152*.[66] It is impossible to know for certain if this ascription was simply the work of the scribe, Charles O'Conor, an educated guess by an intermediate copyist or actually derived from the Book of Kells. If the *notitia* does indeed date from 1152, then it may have been connected with the Synod of Kells held in that year. Muirchertach Ua Briain had clearly set a precedent for using synods as the occasion for granting land to the church (at Cashel in 1101) and Tigernán may similarly have sought to employ the Synod of Kells as the arena for announcing his grant.

At the reforming Synod of Kells the Irish diocesan structure was revised and the archbishoprics of Dublin and Tuam were created and added to those of Armagh and Cashel, which were instituted at the Synod of Ráith Bressail (1111).[67] The Annals of Tigernach and the 17th-century Annals of the Four Masters claim that the synod was held at Droichet Átha,[68] and possibly some of the proceedings took place at Mellifont (Donnchad Ua Cerbaill's Cistercian foundation).[69] Although the 17th-century *Foras feasa ar Éirinn* (one of the main sources for the history of the synod) does not mention a bishopric of Kells, it seems clear from a list made by Cardinal Paparo (who presided over the synod) that such a diocese was established.[70] Unfortunately, no record of the boundary points of this diocese survive.

If Tigernán granted Mag nDechrad to the Columban community in 1152, then it is possible that he may have done so in order to endow the newly created bishopric of Kells. The *notitia* is vague with regard to the identity of the recipients of Tigernán's generosity, it merely states, using a conventional formula, that Mag nDechrad was given *do Dhía et do Cholum Cille* ('to God and to Colum Cille'). It is unclear what the relationship between the Columban community at Kells and the new bishopric was, though it seems that the monastic community did not cease to exist in 1152.[71] With the contraction of Bréifne after the English invasion, Kells lost its episcopal status and much of its land was transferred to the Augustinian priory of St Mary's at some point.[72] In contrast to its accompanying *notitia*, which records that land was donated specifically for the service of the church of Int Ednén, this *notitia* does not indicate the intended function of the land in question.

The gift of Mag nDechrad may have had an element of showmanship to it. Three thousand ecclesiastics attended the synod, according to the Annals of the Four Masters, and Keating claims almost all the bishops of Ireland were in attendance.[73] Such a large gathering of important churchmen would have been a wonderful opportunity for Tigernán to display his largesse towards the church and to the church of Kells in particular, which was one of the sites of the synod. It would also have enabled Tigernán to one-up his rival Donnchad Ua Cerbaill as a supporter of church reform. Ua Cerbaill was the benefactor of the Cistercians at Mellifont, and the Synod of Kells has been described as 'very much a Cistercian affair, indeed the high point of Cistercian influence in the direction of the Irish church'.[74] Ua Cerbaill had been deposed only just before the synod, and this perhaps offered Ua Ruairc the opportunity to steal and don his reforming mantle.[75]

Admittedly the *notitia*'s list of *slána* ('guarantors') does not support this interpretation, in so far as the guarantors are all secular figures (except one) and cannot be linked to the synod. It is not impossible, though ultimately unprovable, that Tigernán may have initially announced the grant at the synod and that the details were later worked out and recorded in the *notitia* after the synod disbanded, hence the lack of synod members as guarantors. Conversely, it is possible that Tigernán's reasons for granting Mag nDechrad in 1152, if indeed it was granted that year, were unrelated to the synod. Both Tigernán and his half-brother, Donnchad Ua Cerbaill, experienced a severe dip in their political fortunes in that year. Donnchad was expelled from the kingship of Airgialla by Muirchertach Mac Lochlainn, ostensibly for a previous attack on Gilla Meic Liaic, archbishop of Armagh, which may have been caused by attempts by Gilla Meic Liaic to regain lands from the diocese of Airgialla for Armagh.[76] By 1152, Tigernán had been in power for 30 years and had repeatedly changed his allegiances, to the point where he was surrounded by enemies. As Ó Corráin has summarized: 'by this time, Ua Ruairc had made himself obnoxious both to O Connor and Mac Murrough. He had played O Connor false on a number of occasions, he was Mac Murrough's chief rival for the spoils of Meath and Mac Lochlainn had little reason to trust him'.[77] Mac Lochlainn and Ua Conchobair, who made a short-lived truce in 1152, briefly joined forces with Diarmait Mac Murchada and partitioned Mide between Murchad Ua Maíl Shechnaill and Máel Sechnaill Ua Maíl Shechnaill, an act which may have involved stripping Tigernán of territory he had gradually acquired during his reign and Mac Lochlainn's partition of Mide two years previously.[78] Furthermore this triumvirate jointly attacked and defeated Tigernán, burning Bun Cuilinn (unidentified) in the process.[79] Finally they stripped Tigernán of Conmaicne (and possibly all of Bréifne) and gave the kingship of Conmaicne (and possibly Bréifne) to the son of Gilla Bruite Ua Ruairc.[80] Injury was added to insult when Mac Murchada also carried off Tigernán's wife, Derbforgaill, with her personal effects.

Tigernán may have had some foreknowledge that Mac Lochlainn and Ua Conchobair were about to turn against him, and indeed he may have realized that the pact Mac Lochlainn and Ua Conchobair's entered into at Mag Ene meant that he could no longer play one off against the other and that they might avenge themselves upon him for his previous faithlessness. In such circumstances Tigernán may have granted Mag nDechrad to the Columban community in an attempt to deny Máel Sechnaill Ua Maíl Shechnaill (to whom the triumvirate granted the territory of Mide which lay to the east of Clonard) the use of this land. Tigernán's grant may have triggered renewed hostilities between Bréifne and Mide, as the later Annals of the Four Masters claim *ro fhás dná, cogadh etir Uí Briúin, ocus Fheraibh Mídhe* ('there arose then a war between Uí Briúin and the men of Mide').[81]

Tigernán's downfall was brief. That same year he gave hostages to Tairdelbach Ua Conchobair in order to obtain Uí Briúin Bréifne (*tar cenn Ua mBriuin*)[82] and again the following year (1153) when Tairdelbach led an army against Mac Murchada and retrieved Derbforgaill.[83] Later that year Tigernán turned against Ua Conchobair, accompanied Mac Lochlainn in battle against him and gave Uí Briúin Bréifne and Conmaicne hostages to Mac Lochlainn. Mac Lochlainn, however, gave all Mide *ó Sionainn co fairrge* ('from Shannon to the sea') to Máel Sechnaill Ua Maíl Shechnaill.[84] It is not clear in this context what lands comprised the kingdom of Mide. It is possible that Tigernán regained much of the former Mide territory that he had accumulated since the start of his reign, thus *ó Sionainn co fairrge*, a variant of the stock phrase mentioned earlier, may not have denoted the Mide of previous centuries. Furthermore, as the phrase defines Mide along an east-west axis, it does not indicate how far north or south Mide extended and therefore may not take the loss of territory in northern Mide into account.

If the grant of Mag nDechrad was not an exercise in damage limitation but occurred after Tigernán's return to power, then it may have been intended as a statement of triumph on the part of Tigernán in late 1152, when he was still in alliance with Ua Conchobair but before he abandoned him for Mac Lochlainn (who granted Mide to Máel Sechnaill). In such circumstances it may have been intended as a visible symbol of his return to power, triumph over of his internal and external rivals and control over former Uí Maíl Shechnaill territory.

Mag nDechrad was given by Tigernán *úadh féin et [o] cech rígh gébhas Brefne co bráth* ('from himself and from every king that shall take Bréifne for ever'). This is the only instance in the *notitiae* where a king is said specifically to bind a grant upon his successors. Furthermore, the grant was made *a comhairle maithe fer mBrefne eter Ua Briúin et Conmaicne co ndola doibh féin i slanaighecht na hedhbarta* ('by the counsel of the nobles of the men of Bréifne both Uí Briúin and Conmaicne, and they themselves went as guarantors for the gift'). This implies that Tigernán was not acting in an arbitrary fashion when he made the grant but had the consent or at least acquiescence of his subordinates. By recording the consent of the nobles of Bréifne to the grant and by including them as guarantors, Tigernán may have sought to use the nobles as a means of ensuring the grant would be honoured by his subordinates and successors.

These provisions suggest that Tigernán may have been concerned with future Bréifne violations of the terms or extent of the grant and not troubled by possible Uí Maíl Shechnaill opposition. To counteract the latter, a general sanction clause, such as that employed in the *notitia* Tigernán witnessed in 1133, could have been employed.[85] The lack of such a clause may suggest that Uí Maíl Shechnaill opposition was not considered a noteworthy possibility. If Tigernán's kingdom was as large as the *notitia* suggests, then Mag nDechrad was within its boundaries and thus outside direct Uí Maíl Shechnaill control. If the grant was made in 1152, when Tigernán may have thought that his position as king of Uí Briúin Bréifne was under pressure, then he may have included the above safeguards in an attempt to prevent hostile branches of Uí Briúin Bréifne, such as Uí Ragallaig who held lands in the neighbourhood of Kells, from acquiring a base in former Mide territory from which to threaten his position. In such circumstances, however, given the repeated partitioning of Mide, Tigernán may have expected Ua Conchobair and Mac Lochlainn to strip Uí Briúin Bréifne of its Mide territory. If this were so, it would matter little whether the Bréifne nobility sanctioned the grant or not. The grant, therefore, should be read with the understanding that Tigernán was acting from a position of security and not uncertainty. As such, the two statements, *úadh féin et [o] cech rígh gébhas Brefne co bráth* and *a comhairle maithe fer mBrefne eter Ua Briúin et Conmaicne co ndola doibh féin i slanaighecht na hedhbarta*, were most likely included by Tigernán to assert and emphasize his control over Uí Briúin and Conmaicne.

THE GUARANTORS

The law tracts of the 7th and 8th centuries show that contracts and agreements in early medieval Ireland were supported by a complex system of suretyship, but the technical vocabulary that surrounds it appears to be absent from this *notitia*, perhaps indicating that much of it was already obsolete.[86] Instead, *slána* ('guarantors'), a more generalized term that was increasingly popular from the Middle Irish period onwards, is applied to those who stood in support of the gift. Since the nobles of Bréifne and Conmaicne are said to have acted as guarantors and the subsequent sentence in the *notitia* introduces the guarantors, it implies that all those named were counted among the nobility of those territories. Máire Herbert has suggested that this implies that the grant was formalized in Tigernán's territory.[87] As in Tigernán's other grant, members of the community of Kells are notable for their absence and no secular titles are ascribed to any of the guarantors.

The first two guarantors, Gofraid Ua Ragallaig and Lorcán Ua Donnchada were from Muintir Maíl Mórda (see Fig. 1).[88] Gofraid appears in the Uí Ragallaig genealogies as an ancestor of Clann an Chaoich, who gave their name to the barony of Clankee in Co. Cavan.[89] Clankee borders on the baronies of Lower Kells and Morgallion (which derives its name from the Gailenga) to the south. This, in conjunction with the title the Annals of Tigernach bestowed upon Gofraid at his death, *rí Muntire Mael Mordha ocus Muighe Gaileng* ('king of Muintir Maíl Mórda and Mag Gaileng'), suggests that Gofraid's chief interests lay in the neighbourhood of Kells, and he was subsequently killed there by Tigernán's son, Máel Sechnaill, in 1161.[90] Previously Gofraid had been banished to Connacht following a failed revolt in 1154, he forcibly released Donnchad Ua Cerbaill from imprisonment by Ua Ruairc in 1155, and a spate of Uí Ruairc-Uí Ragallaig killings of the early 1160s all indicate that the relationship between Tigernán and Gofraid was increasingly poisonous after 1154.[91] It is therefore likely that the grant of Mag nDechrad occurred prior to 1154, as they were probably not on good terms after that date.

Lorcán Ua Donnchada does not feature in either the annalistic or genealogical records. Mac Niocaill hazarded a guess that he may have been a brother of Cennétig Ua Donnchada, who appeared as a guarantor of Tigernán's grant to Int Ednén.[92] It is impossible to say whether this was so, although it seems reasonable to assume that they were related, since both Cennétig and Lorcán were stated in the *notitiae* to be members of Muintir Maíl Mórda. An unnamed Ua Donnchada is recorded as falling in battle against the English in 1171, whereas Uí Ragallaig sided with the invaders against Uí Ruairc, which may suggest that Lorcán's (or at least his family's) primary allegiance was to Tigernán rather than Gofraid (or eventually became so).[93] If inclusion in the guarantor list is taken as a sign of contemporary importance, Tigernán may have been attempting to show favour to Uí Donnchada and promote them at the expense of their Muintir Maíl Mórda kinsmen, Uí Ragallaig. Alternatively, if the grant was an attempt by Tigernán to express dominance over disgruntled factions within his kingdom, the guarantor list may not have been a simple roll call of political favourites but each individual may have been included, for separate reasons, in order to secure the grant. For example, Lorcán may have been included as a sign of favour but Gofraid Ua Ragallaig's inclusion may have been intended to emphasize his subordination to Tigernán's desire to grant a large expanse of land to Kells that Gofraid may have had designs upon.

Gilla Pátraic, grandson of Fiachra, from Clann Chathail also defies positive identification. Mac Niocaill posited that Gilla Pátraic may have been a brother of Amlaíb, grandson of Fiachra from Clann Chathail, who is mentioned in the Int Ednén *notitia*.[94] Again, as in the case of Lorcán and Cennétig Ua Donnchada, there is no definitive proof of consanguinity but it is a reasonable assumption. Who this Clann Chathail were is also an open question, but it possible that they were the same Clann Chathail that were a branch of Síl Muiredaig of Connacht (from which the ruling Uí Chonchobair also sprung), and were located around Elphin, Co. Roscommon (see Fig. 1). If so, they offer evidence to suggest that Tigernán was cultivating friends west of the Shannon, within Uí Chonchobair's traditional heartlands, as befitted an ambitious *ardri Airthir Connacht*.

The next guarantor, Ímar son of Tigernán, from Cenél Brénainn, is the only contemporary person, apart from Tigernán Ua Ruairc himself, to appear in both of Tigernán's grants. The Cenél Brénainn were probably one of the lesser ruling families of Bréifne, and appear in the late 13th-century annals in association with Tellach nDúnchadha (barony of Tullyhunco, Co. Cavan), although it cannot be said for certain they were present there during the first half of the 12th century.[95] Nonetheless, Ímar, who was probably a member of Meic Tigearnáin of Tellach nDúnchadha, was of sufficient importance to be included in both *notitiae*. It may be possible that Ímar had influential, albeit distant, ecclesiastical connections, as Brénainn, ancestor of Cenél Brénainn, was an ancestor of Tuathal Ua Connachtaig (*ob.*1179), bishop of Uí Briúin, who attended the Synod of Kells,[96] and of Uí Dhubthaig, a powerful 12th-century ecclesiastical family in Bréifne and Connacht.[97]

The final guarantor, Gilla Ciaráin Ua Draignén, was *comarba Féchín* ('successor of Féchín'). Féchín (who is said to have died *c.*665) was patron of the monastery of Fobar (Fore), which gives its name to the baronies of Fore in Meath and Westmeath, and which appears to have been an important monastery, featuring regularly in the annals between the 7th and 12th centuries. Féchín was considered a member of the Luigne of Connacht, who were believed to be related to the Luigne of the midlands, and who along with the Gailenga of Brega (in and around Kells) came under increasing Uí Briúin Bréifne influence during the 11th and 12th centuries.[98] In the surviving Irish Life of Féchín, which dates from 1329, the saint appears repeatedly in contact with Síl nÁeda Sláine kings of Brega.[99] The presence of *comarba Féchín* as a guarantor in the record of this 12th-century Uí Ruairc grant, however, is indicative of the extension of Uí Ruairc authority into territory previously dominated by the Southern Uí Néill.[100]

Tigernán's interest in Fobar may have been linked to his increasing influence over Kells. As noted above, Gilla Ciaráin Ua Draignén had probably been *comarba* since the death of Mac Gilla Fhionáin Ua Ciblecháin in 1137.[101] Another *notitia*, which can be dated to between 1134 and 1136, records that Flann Ua Ciblecháin held the position of *secnab* in Kells.[102] This is the only appearance of this office in the *notitiae* and Flann appears second to last in the list of Kells officials, which may suggest that the office of *secnab* was not of huge significance in the 12th century.[103] Nevertheless, the presence of two Uí Chiblecháin in Kells and Fobar during the 1130s suggests a connection between the two communities at the time. This link may be reflected in the Life of Féchín, as it was Columba who was said to have prophesied the coming of Féchín to Fobar.[104] Uí Draignén, the family of the new *comarba*, were members of the Laigin according to 12th-century Laigin genealogies: *Úi Draignén h-i Fobur* are recorded as descendants of Conall mac Echach, progenitor of Uí Garrchon.[105] Uí Garrchon had fallen from power in Laigin during the 6th century but a number of important Laigin saints, such as Cóemgein of Glendalough and Conláed of Kildare, were of their line.[106] The inclusion of Gilla Ciaráin Ua Draignén as a guarantor of Tigernán's grant may be indicative not just of Uí Ruairc penetration of Southern Uí Néill territory, but also of his rivalry with Donnchad Ua Cerbaill. As seen earlier, Donnchad had introduced the Arrouasian Augustinians to Termonn Féichín (a pre-existing church dedicated to Féchín), probably during the 1140s. The presence of *comarba Féchín* in Tigernán's *notitia* may have been a statement of the superiority of his ecclesiastical connections and influence over those of Donnchad.

CONCLUSION

The record of the grant of Mag nDechrad, when viewed in its probable ecclesiastical and political context, provides an insight into the ambitions and rivalries which engaged Tigernán Ua Ruairc. The generosity involved in the donation of such a large area does not disguise the fact that this gift was a calculated act, which was probably intended to fulfill a number of purposes. The strategic location of Mag nDechrad meant that it could act as a partial buffer between Uí Briúin Bréifne and enemies such as Uí Maíl Shechnaill. The endowment of Kells, the seat of a new episcopal see for Tigernán's kingdom, with sufficient territory appropriate to its status, may have been important to Tigernán's prestige. Furthermore, the gift may also have been prompted by the intense political competition engaged in by various 12th-century kings, as it allowed Tigernán to pose as an ecclesiastical benefactor as mighty and benevolent as his rival Donnchad Ua Cerbaill, or would-be superiors Tairdelbach Ua Conchobair and Muirchertach Mac Lochlainn.

Conclusion

The *notitiae* provide a unique insight into the actions and motivations of Uí Ruairc and Uí Maíl Shechnaill kings during the 11th and 12th centuries, as seen through their property connections with the wealthy church of Kells. Even though a rough chronology of these kings' activities may be reconstructed from surviving annals, the *notitiae* offer the rare opportunity to view individual acts of statecraft in action. In particular, the record of the grant of Mag nDechrad, when viewed in its probable ecclesiastical and political context, casts light upon the ambitions and rivalries which engaged Tigernán Ua Ruairc, and is valuable for elucidating the history of the midlands (and particularly the greater Kells area) in the middle of the 12th century.

Likewise, the *notitiae* seem to indicate that the church of Kells too sought alliance with the rising Uí Briúin Bréifne (both Uí Ruairc and Uí Ragallaig), who were beginning to overshadow Kells' older sponsors, Uí Maíl Shechnaill of Clann Cholmáin. The Kells *notitiae* record four grants of land by three different kings during the 11th and 12th centuries; the first two by 11th-century Uí Maíl Shechnaill kings.[1] These were a grant of immunity over the church of Kildalkey to the community of Kells (between 1033 and 1040)[2] and a grant of a *dísert* ('retreat', lit. 'desert') for the use of pilgrims in Kells (between 1073 and 1084).[3] However, by the second quarter of the 12th century it was Uí Briúin Bréifne – and more specifically Tigernán Ua Ruairc – to whom the community of Kells looked for support. His grant of land for the service of the church of Int Ednén (between 1122 and 1148) and grant of Mag nDechrad to the community of Kells (between 1137 and 1161, probably *c.*1152) point to the eclipse of the Uí Maíl Shechnaill as Kells' primary political patrons and it is perhaps a measure of this that when the king of Mide, Murchad Ua Maíl Shechnaill, died in the year after the grant of Mag nDechrad (1153), he breathed his last at Durrow – Kells was already beyond his grasp.

It is apparent that each grant recorded in the *notitiae* was enacted within specific political contexts, in which the mutual benefit of both donors and recipients were carefully considered. The *notitiae* bear witness to the use of land as a political tool, and although possession of land appears to have been a prerequisite for the accumulation of wealth and the exercise of power, so too kings could benefit from alienating land and land rights. For example, Ua Ruairc's grant to Int Ednén was probably intended to ingratiate himself with Kells, while his grant of Mag nDechrad (a substantial philanthropic enterprise in its own right) may have helped shield his kingdom from attack from the south and east. The donation of strategically located sites to the church (in order to impede attacks) was also part of the *modus operandi* of other kings and Donnchad Ua Cerbaill's foundation of Mellifont – so spectacularly celebrated on the consecration of its new church in 1157 – acted as a buffer for his recently-expanded southern border too.

Beyond the exploits of great kings, the *notitiae* in the Book of Kells offer historians the opportunity to explore a variety of concerns. To date scholars have mainly concerned themselves with defining what the *notitiae* are and where they fit into historic documentary trends, rather than with what the texts say. Study of the contents of the *notitiae* may yet yield much information about Irish society in the 11th and 12th centuries. For example, they may be used, in conjunction with other sources such as the annals, as a means of investigating 11th- and 12th-century Irish economic conditions. They are, after all, records of financial transactions, and indicate that a mixture of currencies (cattle, gold, silver and coin) were current in 11th- and 12th-century Kells, while also being witnesses to other economic factors, such as the inflationary effects of plagues, like the cattle murrain that occurred in 1133.[4]

In short, while the Book of Kells might well be one of our most important national treasures on account of its splendid artistry, from the perspective of a historian of medieval Irish kingship or of the locality of Kells, it too justifies its description as *primh-mind iarthair domain* – 'the most precious object of the western world',[5] not for being the 'work of angels' but for what it tells us about the work of men.

Notes

ABBREVIATIONS

AClon   Denis Murphy (ed.), *The annals of Clonmacnoise being annals of Ireland from the earliest period to AD 1408; translated into English AD 1627 by Conell Mageoghagan* (Dublin, 1896).

AFM   John O'Donovan (ed. and trans.), *Annála ríoghachta Éireann: annals of the kingdom of Ireland by the Four Masters, from the earliest period to the year 1616* (7 vols, 2nd ed., Dublin, 1856).

AI   Seán Mac Airt (ed. and trans.), *The annals of Inisfallen (MS Rawlinson B. 503)* (Dublin, 1951).

ALC   William Hennessy (ed. and trans.), *The annals of Loch Cé* (2 vols, London, 1871).

ATig   Whitley Stokes (ed. and trans.), 'The annals of Tigernach', *Revue Celtique*, 16 (1895), 374–419; 17 (1896), 6–33, 119–263 and 337–420 and 18 (1897), 9–59, 150–97 and 267–303. Gearóid Mac Niocaill (trans.), *The annals of Tigernach*, https://celt.ucc.ie/published/T100002A/index.html (accessed 2 July 2019).

AU   Seán Mac Airt and Gearóid Mac Niocaill (eds and trans), *The annals of Ulster (to AD 1131). Part 1: text and translation* (Dublin, 1983).

AU²   William Hennessy and Brian MacCarthy (eds and trans), *Annála Uladh, annals of Ulster otherwise annála Senait, annals of Senat: a chronicle of Irish affairs from AD 432 to AD 1540* (4 vols, Dublin, 1887–1901).

CGH   M.A. O'Brien (ed.), *Corpus genealogiarum Hiberniae* (Dublin, 1962).

CS   Gearóid Mac Niocaill (ed. and trans.), *Chronicon Scotorum*, http://www.ucc.ie/celt/published/G100016/index.html (edition), http://www.ucc.ie/celt/published/T100016/index.html (translation) (accessed 2 July 2019).

Misc   Séamus Ó hInnse (ed. and trans.), *Miscellaneous Irish annals (AD 1114–1437)* (Dublin, 1947).

NHI, i   Dáibhí Ó Cróinín (ed.), *A new history of Ireland, i: prehistoric and early Ireland* (Oxford, 2005).

ob.   *obit* (year of death)

ODNB   H.C.G. Matthew and Brian Harrison (eds), *Oxford dictionary of national biography* (60 vols, Oxford, 2004).

s.a.   *sub anno* (under year)

s.v.   *sub verbo/verbis* (under word/words)

A NOTE ON THE ANNALS

The annals – which are the main sources for events and chronology of medieval Irish history – will be cited by siglum, year and entry number of their printed editions, e.g. the reference to the entry in the Annals of Ulster under 1007 describing the theft of the Book of Kells is given as *AU* 1007.11. (The exception to this practice will be the Annals of Tigernach, which are cited by the year and entry number of the online translation by Gearóid Mac Niocaill, and not Whitley Stokes' printed edition). In some texts the dating of events is several years out from the actual years in which they occurred and/or entries are not given individual numbers; where this occurs the text is cited *sub anno* (under year), for example the Annals of Ulster and

Annals of the Four Masters entries on the 802 Viking attack on Iona are cited as *AU* 802.9 and *AFM s.a.* 797. Entries for the same event are grouped together, and where multiple events are cited, a semicolon is used to separate them.

INTRODUCTION

1   *AU²* s.a. 1172.
2   The edition and translation of these *notitiae* that will be used in this study is Gearóid Mac Niocaill (ed. and trans.), 'The Irish "Charters"' in Peter Fox (ed.), *The Book of Kells: MS 58 Trinity College library Dublin* (Lucerne, 1990), pp 153–65.
3   On the various later additions to the manuscript, see Bernard Meehan, *The Book of Kells* (London, 2012), pp 26–8. I am grateful to Dr Meehan for the gift of a copy of his book.
4   Marie Therese Flanagan, *The transformation of the Irish church in the twelfth and thirteenth centuries* (Woodbridge, 2010), p. 164.
5   A good example of this may be seen in a text entered into the 9th-century Book of Armagh on behalf of Brian Boru (*ob.*1014): Denis Casey, 'Brian Boru, the Book of Armagh and the Irish church in the tenth and eleventh centuries' in Seán Duffy (ed.), *Medieval Dublin XVI. Proceedings of Clontarf 1014–2014: national conference marking the millennium of the Battle of Clontarf* (Dublin, 2017), pp 103–21.
6   Patrick Wormald, 'Celtic and Anglo-Saxon kingship: some further thoughts' in Paul E. Szarmach and Virginia Darrow Oggins (eds), *Sources of Anglo-Saxon culture: papers from the symposium on the sources of Anglo-Saxon culture held in conjunction with the eighteenth international congress on medieval studies at Western Michigan University, May 5–8, 1983* (Kalamazoo, MN, 1986), p. 152.

I. LAND IN MEDIEVAL IRELAND

1   Colin Ireland (ed. and trans.), *Old Irish wisdom attributed to Aldfrith of Northumbria: an edition of* Bríathra Flainn Fhína maic Ossu (Tempe, AZ, 1999), pp 88–9 (§6.87). Although Flann Fína/Aldfrith died in 705, the extant text dates from the 8th/9th century.
2   Gearóid Mac Niocaill (ed. and trans.), 'Tír Cumaile', *Ériu*, 22 (1971), 81–6.

3   Fergus Kelly, *Early Irish farming: a study based mainly on the law-texts of the 7th and 8th centuries AD* (Dublin, 2000).
4   Ibid., pp 423–4.
5   Kuno Meyer (ed. and trans.), *The triads of Ireland* (Dublin, 1906), pp 22–3 (§167). The advantages of land ownership are also praised: ibid., pp 8–9 (§§72–3). See also praise of proprietorship in the 9th-century *Tecosca Cormaic*: Kuno Meyer (ed. and trans.), *The instructions of king Cormac mac Airt* (Dublin, 1909), pp 46–7 (§31).
6   Kuno Meyer (ed. and trans.), Betha Cholmáin maic Lúacháin: *Life of Colmán son of Lúachan. Edited from a manuscript in the library of Rennes, with translation, introduction, notes, and indices* (Dublin, 1911).
7   Charles Doherty, 'Ruaidrí ua Canannáin' in *ODNB*.
8   For a discussion of the political geography of Donegal, see Brian Lacey, *Cenél Conaill and the Donegal kingdoms, AD500–800* (Dublin, 2006), pp 49–144. Ua Domnaill of Cenél Lugdach eventually monopolized the kingship of Cenél Conaill from the 13th century onwards, but their rise owed much to Scots, Norman and Cenél nEógain activity: F.J. Byrne, 'Ireland and her neighbours, *c.*1014–*c.*1072' in *NHI*, i, pp 881–2.
9   For the rise of Dál Cais, see Máire Ní Mhaonaigh, *Brian Boru: Ireland's greatest king?* (Stroud, 2007), pp 15–28.
10 For Eóganacht resurgence, see ibid., pp 116–18 and Marie Therese Flanagan, 'High-kings with opposition, 1072–1166' in *NHI*, i, pp 918–22.
11 *CS s.a.* 823.
12 *AFM s.a.* 1072, *AClon s.a.* 1069; *AFM s.a.* 1076.
13 *AU²* s.a. 1177.
14 Myles Dillon (ed. and trans.), *Lebor na cert: the book of rights* (Dublin, 1962), pp 44–7 and Whitley Stokes (ed. and trans.), 'The death of Crimthann, son of Fidach, and the adventures of the sons of Eochaid Muigmedón', *Revue Celtique*, 24 (1903), 186–7.

15 In the middle of the 9th century the humiliated king of Munster was forced to acknowledge the alienation of the kingdom of Osraige (mainly modern Co. Kilkenny) to Leth Cuinn (the northern half of Ireland, which was dominated by the Uí Néill): *AU* 859.3, *CS* s.a. 859 and *AFM* s.a. 857. The later Fragmentary Annals, which were probably compiled during the reign of Donnchad mac Gilla Pátraic (*ob.*1039), ignore Munster involvement in this act. They downplay the event by saying that Cerball, king of Osraige, simply submitted to Máel Sechnaill, king of Tara, in obedience to Fethgna, *comarba Pátraic* (spiritual heir of St Patrick, i.e., head of the church of Armagh) and not that his kingdom had been treated as a political football by the Clann Cholmáin king of Tara: Joan Radner (ed. and trans.), *Fragmentary annals of Ireland* (Dublin, 1978), pp 106–7 (§268).

16 Denis Casey, 'Studies in the exercise of royal power in Ireland, *c.*650–*c.*1200AD' (PhD, University of Cambridge, 2009), pp 126–32.

17 Mac Niocaill, 'Irish "Charters"', pp 160–1 (§8(i)). For a detailed discussion of this grant see Denis Casey, 'Tigernán Ua Ruairc and the Book of Kells' in Katharine Simms (ed.), *Gaelic Ireland (c.600–c.1700): politics, culture and landscapes; studies for the 'Irish Chiefs' prize* (Dublin, 2013), pp 3–10. For a briefer discussion, see Denis Casey, '"A man of great power for a long time": Tigernán Ua Ruairc and the Book of Kells', *History Ireland*, 18:5 (Sept./Oct. 2010), 14–17.

18 *CS* s.a. 1096 and *AFM* s.a. 1096.

19 *AU²* s.a. 1165. This might also be translated as 'through the grace/gift of the kingship of Ua [Mac] Lochlainn'.

20 Charles Doherty, 'Exchange and trade in early medieval Ireland', *Journal of the Royal Society of Antiquaries of Ireland*, 110 (1980), 67–8.

21 Thomas Charles-Edwards, 'A contract between king and people in early medieval Ireland? *Críth gablach* on kingship', *Peritia*, 8 (1994), 111–12.

22 Fergus Kelly, *A guide to early Irish law* (Dublin, 1988), pp 26–7. According to the law texts, the typical fief advanced by the lord consisted mainly of livestock.

On occasion, however, the lord may have given land as part of the fief. For example, see D.A. Binchy (ed.), *Críth gablach* (Dublin, 1941), pp 4–5 (§10).

23 J.G. O'Keeffe (ed. and trans.), 'The rule of Patrick', *Ériu*, 1 (1904), 219 and 222–3 (§9). Similarly the term *frithfholad* is used in an Old Irish list of aphorisms to suggest that even the lowliest of landholders has rights: *Dligid fuidir frithfholta* ('A *fuidir* is entitled to counter obligations'): Ireland, *Old Irish wisdom attributed to Aldfrith of Northumbria*, pp 70–1 (§3.8). For the legal status of *fuidir*, see Kelly, *Guide to early Irish law*, pp 33–5.

24 J.G. O'Keeffe (ed.), '*Dál Caladbuig*' in John Fraser, Paul Grosjean and J.G. O'Keeffe (eds), *Irish Texts* 1 (London, 1931), pp 19–21.

25 Dillon, *Lebor na cert*.

26 Charles Plummer (ed. and trans.), *Bethada náem nÉrenn: Lives of Irish saints* (2 vols, Oxford, 1922), i, p. 288. My translation.

27 Mac Niocaill, 'Irish "Charters"', p. 159 (§6). Denis Casey, '"A compulsory and burdensome imposition": billeting soldiers in medieval and early modern Ireland' in Albrecht Classen and Nadia Margolis (eds), *War and peace: critical issues in European societies and literature, 800–1800* (Berlin, 2011), pp 193–216.

2. TIGERNÁN UA RUAIRC AND THE CHURCH OF KELLS

1 *Misc* 1165.3. William Hennessy and David Kelly (eds and trans), *The Book of Fenagh* (Dublin, 1875), pp 64–5. Geoffrey Keating, *Foras feasa ar Éirinn le Seathrún Céitinn, D.D.*, eds and trans David Comyn and Pádraig Dinneen (4 vols, London, 1901–13), iii, pp 318–21. Gerald of Wales, *Expugnatio Hibernica: the conquest of Ireland by Giraldus Cambrensis*, eds and trans A.B. Scott and F.X. Martin (Dublin, 1978), pp 24–7 (§1.1). Evelyn Mullally (ed. and trans.), *The deeds of the Normans in Ireland* (La geste des Engleis en Yrlande): *a new edition of the chronicle formerly known as* The song of Dermot and the Earl (Dublin, 2002), pp 53–9.

2 *AU* 1128.5; *AU²* s.a. 1172.

3 Meyer, *Triads*, p. 6 (§58).

4   F.J. Byrne, *Irish kings and high-kings* (revised ed., Dublin, 2001), p. xxviii.

5   *CGH*, p. 175. It would appear strange that the Book of Leinster, a manuscript heavily associated with Tigernán's antagonist Diarmait Mac Murchada, should contain such an anomaly, unless it was an attempt to make a (now obscure) dig at Tigernán's parentage?

6   Colin Veach, 'Henry II's grant of Meath to Hugh de Lacy in 1172: a reassessment', *Ríocht na Mídhe*, 18 (2007), 77.

7   Scott and Martin, *Expugnatio Hibernica*, pp 24–5 (§1.1), 84–5 (§1.24) and 90–1 (§1.29).

8   Mullally, *Deeds of the Normans in Ireland*, p. 53.

9   Veach, 'Henry II's grant of Meath to Hugh de Lacy', 77.

10 For biographies of Tigernán, see Marie Therese Flanagan, 'Ua Ruairc, Tigernán' in *ODNB* and Ailbhe Mac Shamhráin, 'Ua Ruairc, Tigernán' in James McGuire and James Quinn (eds), *Dictionary of Irish biography from the earliest times to the year 2002* (9 vols, Cambridge, 2009), ix, pp 600–2.

11 Meyer, *Triads*, pp 2–3 (§7). *Áinius* might also be translated as 'splendour' or 'delightfulness' and in a religious sense could be applied to the bliss of heaven: *Electronic Dictionary of the Irish Language*, *s.v. áinius* (http://www.dil.ie/1424) (accessed 2 July 2019).

12 Thomas Charles-Edwards, *Early Christian Ireland* (Cambridge, 2000), p. 15.

13 Nathalie Stalmans and Thomas Charles-Edwards, 'Saints of Meath' in *ODNB*.

14 For a useful and well-illustrated discussion of this region, see Conor Newman, 'Re-composing the archaeological landscape of Tara' in Edel Bhreathnach (ed.), *The kingship and landscape of Tara* (Dublin, 2005), pp 361–409.

15 Catherine Swift, '*Óenach Tailten*, the Blackwater valley and the Uí Néill kings of Tara' in Alfred P. Smyth (ed.), *Seanchas: studies in early and medieval Irish archaeology, history and literature in honour of Francis J. Byrne* (Dublin, 2000), pp 112–13. Catherine Swift, 'The local context of *Óenach Tailten*', *Ríocht na Mídhe*, 11 (2000), 26–8.

16 David Greene (ed.), Fingal Rónáin *and other stories* (Dublin, 1955), pp 29 and 31. *CGH*, p. 70.

17 William Hennessy (ed. and trans.), 'The battle of Cnucha', *Revue Celtique*, 2 (1873–5), 86–7.

18 Kuno Meyer (ed.), 'Mitteilungen aus irischen Handschriften', *Zeitschrift für celtische Philologie*, 7 (1910), 306.

19 Whitley Stokes (ed. and trans.), *Lives of saints from the Book of Lismore* (Oxford, 1890), pp 28 and 176.

20 F.J. Byrne, 'Church and politics, *c*.750–*c*.1100' in *NHI, i*, p. 665.

21 Ludwig Bieler (ed. and trans.), *The Patrician texts in the Book of Armagh* (Dublin, 1979), pp 146–7 (§27).

22 The suggestion in the Irish Historic Towns Atlas that there was an Iron-Age *dún* at Kells also seems unlikely: Anngret Simms and Katharine Simms, *Kells* (Dublin, 1990), p. 1.

23 Charles-Edwards, *Early Christian Ireland*, p. 555.

24 Ibid.

25 Ibid., p. 554.

26 For a discussion of Fíachu's involvement in Uí Néill expansion see ibid., pp 449–53 and 458.

27 This can be demonstrated by the obit dates of their patrons: Brendan of Birr (*ob*.565/73) and Áed mac Bricc of Rahugh (*ob*.586). Although Mo Chutu of Rahan (*ob*.637) died in the 7th century, his cult seems to have replaced that of Camulacus, an earlier 6th-century British saint, see Stalmans and Charles-Edwards, 'Saints of Meath'. Fínán of Kinnitty may also be added to this list as he flourished during the late 6th/early 7th century. Colmán Elo of Lynally died in the early 7th century (*ob*.611), although Lynally may also have been founded in the 6th century.

28 Charles Doherty, 'Some aspects of hagiography as a source for Irish economic history', *Peritia*, 1 (1982), 309–10.

29 Máire Herbert, *Iona, Kells and Derry: the history and hagiography of the monastic* Familia *of Columba* (Oxford, 1988), pp 68–9.

30 *AU* 807.4.

31 Simms and Simms, *Kells*, p. 1.

32 Herbert, *Iona, Kells and Derry*, p. 68.

33 Three attacks on Iona are recorded prior to the foundation of Kells: *AI* 795.2; *AU* 802.9, *AFM s.a.* 797; *AU* 806.8, *CS s.a.* 806 and *AFM s.a.* 801. The 795 entry in the Annals of Inisfallen reports the plundering of Iona, Inis Muiredaig and Inis Bó Finne. As none of these attacks were recorded in any other chronicle, this entry may have been incorrect or misplaced, and so only two attacks may have occurred.

34 The title abbot of Iona was still recorded in the annals and some of these abbots probably divided their time between Kells and Iona, such as Cellach (*ob.*815), who built the church of Kells and his successor Diarmait, who travelled between Scotland and Ireland with the relics of Columba in 818 and 831: *CS s.a.* 818, *AFM s.a.* 816; *CS s.a.* 831, *AU* 831.1. Diarmait's successor, Innrechtach, appears to have been a resident of Iona, as he too brought relics of Columba to Ireland: *AU* 849.7.

35 For example Donnchad mac Domnaill (*ob.*797) had the support of the community of Durrow in battle: *AU* 776.11.

36 Herbert, *Iona, Kells, and Derry*, p. 69.

37 *AU* 743.3.

38 Byrne, 'Church and politics', p. 664.

39 Herbert, *Iona, Kells, and Derry*, p. 70. The site itself may have been located at the eastern end of the territory of the Caílle Follamain, who claimed descent from Colmán Becc, brother of the Clann Cholmáin ancestor Colmán Már (and possibly a genealogical duplicate of him): Paul MacCotter, *Medieval Ireland: territorial, political and economic divisions* (Dublin, 2008), p. 203.

40 Charles Doherty has suggested that the land for Kells was donated by Armagh, but this too seems speculative: 'Warrior and king in early Ireland' in Jan Erik Rekdal and Charles Doherty (eds), *Kings and warriors in early north-west Europe* (Dublin, 2016), 96–8.

41 Ibid. *AU* 814.9.

42 Máire Herbert and Pádraig Ó Riain (eds and trans), *Betha Adamnáin* (London and Cork, 1988).

43 *AU* 920.6, *CS s.a.* 920, *AFM s.a.* 918 and *AClon s.a.* 916.

44 *AU* 951.3 and *CS s.a.* 951.

45 *CS s.a.* 970; *AU* 997.3; *ATig* 1019.3, *CS s.a.* 1019 and *AFM s.a.* 1018. The relationships between the Vikings and the dominant Clann Cholmáin are teased out in Eoin O'Flynn, 'The Dublin Vikings and the Clann Cholmáin kings of the Southern Uí Néill' in Seán Duffy (ed.), *Medieval Dublin XIII: proceedings of the Friends of Medieval Dublin symposium 2011* (Dublin, 2013), pp 13–26.

46 *AU* 904.2.

47 Herbert, *Iona, Kells and Derry*, pp 78–89. For the early 11th century as the turning point in the transfer of jurisdiction, see Thomas Owen Clancy, 'Iona v. Kells: succession, jurisdiction and politics in the Columban *Familia* in the later tenth century' in Fiona Edmonds and Paul Russell (eds), *Tome: studies in medieval Celtic history and law in honour of Thomas Charles-Edwards* (Woodbridge, 2011), pp 89–101.

48 Mac Niocaill, 'Irish "Charters"', pp 157–8 (§4).

49 Herbert, *Iona, Kells and Derry*, p. 125.

50 Bairbre Nic Aongusa, 'The monastic hierarchy in twelfth-century Ireland: the case of Kells', *Ríocht na Mídhe*, 8 (1987–93), 16–17. For a discussion of the urban characteristics of settlements such as Kells which support Nic Aongusa's view, see Charles Doherty, 'The monastic town in early medieval Ireland' in Howard Clarke and Anngret Simms (eds), *The comparative history of urban origins in non-Roman Europe: Ireland, Wales, Denmark, Germany, Poland and Russia from the ninth to the thirteenth century* (Oxford, 1985), pp 45–75.

51 Mary Valante, 'Reassessing the Irish "monastic town"', *Irish Historical Studies*, 31:1 (May 1998), 1–18.

52 Colmán Etchingham, *The Irish 'monastic town': is this a valid concept?* (Cambridge, 2010).

3. THE ROYAL GRANTS IN THE BOOK OF KELLS

1 Gearóid Mac Niocaill (ed.), *Notitiae as Leabhar Cheanannais, 1033–1161* (Dublin, 1961), p. 5. My translation.

2 See for example David Dumville, *Liturgy and the ecclesiastical history of late Anglo-Saxon*

England: four studies (Woodbridge, 1992),
pp 120–3.

3   Dauvit Broun, *The charters of Gaelic
Scotland and Ireland in the early and central
Middle Ages* (Cambridge, 1995), p. 32.

4   The most recent edition and translation
of the *notitiae* in the Book of Deer is
Katherine Forsyth, Dauvit Broun and
Thomas Clancy (eds and trans), 'The
property records: text and translation'
in Katherine Forsyth (ed.), *Studies on the
Book of Deer* (Dublin, 2008), pp 131–44.
For the lone *notitia* in the Book of
Durrow, see Richard Irvine Best (ed.
and trans.), 'An early monastic grant in
the Book of Durrow', *Ériu*, 10 (1928),
137–9.

5   Interestingly, the surviving portions of
other prominent manuscripts associated
closely with Columba, such as the
Cathach, contain no comparable records.

6   John O'Donovan (ed. and trans.), 'The
Irish charters in the Book of Kells', *The
Miscellany of the Irish Archaeological Society*,
1 (1846), p. 150.

7   Máire Herbert, 'Charter material from
Kells' in Felicity O'Mahony (ed.), *The
Book of Kells: proceedings of a conference at
Trinity College Dublin, 6–9 September 1992*
(Aldershot, 1994), pp 61–2.

8   Dumville, *Liturgy and the ecclesiastical
history*, p. 119. This may not necessarily
apply to the Gaelic examples, although
it could be argued that the first *notitia*
in the Book of Deer – as it contained
Deer's foundation legend involving
Columba – had a similar liturgical value
as a saint's Life: Kenneth Jackson (ed. and
trans.), *The Gaelic notes in the Book of Deer*
(Cambridge, 1972), pp 30 and 32 (§1).

9   Jackson, *Gaelic notes in the Book of
Deer*, pp 89–91. For the latter, see the
discussion of Cambridge, Corpus
Christi College, MS 140 in Neil R. Ker,
*Catalogue of manuscripts containing Anglo-
Saxon* (Oxford, 1957), p. 47 (§35).

10 Dumville, *Liturgy and the ecclesiastical
history*, p. 126.

11 Jackson, *Gaelic notes in the Book of Deer*,
pp 1–7.

12 Thomas Clancy, 'Deer and the early
church in north-eastern Scotland' in
Forsyth (ed.), *Studies on the Book of Deer*,
pp 363–4.

13 Alan Orr Anderson and Marjorie Ogilvie
Anderson (eds and trans), *Adomnán's Life
of Columba* (revised ed., Oxford, 1991),
pp 24–7 (§1.3).

14 Herbert, *Iona, Kells and Derry*, pp 71 and
94.

15 Ibid., pp 101 and 106.

16 Ibid., p. 79.

17 Richard Sharpe, 'Dispute settlement in
medieval Ireland: a preliminary inquiry'
in Wendy Davies and Paul Fouracre (eds),
*The settlement of disputes in early medieval
Europe* (Cambridge, 1986), pp 173–4.

18 Herbert, *Iona, Kells and Derry*, p. 124.

19 Broun, *Charters of Gaelic Scotland and
Ireland*, pp 34–7.

20 Mac Niocaill, 'Irish "Charters"',
pp 153–4 and Mac Niocaill, *Notitiae as
Leabhar Cheanannais*, p. 2.

21 Mac Niocaill, 'Irish "Charters"', p. 154.

22 Standish O'Grady, Robin Flower
and Myles Dillon, *Catalogue of Irish
manuscripts in the British Museum* (3 vols,
London, 1926–53), i, p. 1.

23 Nessa Ní Shéaghdha and Pádraig Ó
Macháin, *Catalogue of Irish manuscripts
in the National Library of Ireland* (13 vols,
Dublin, 1961–96), ix, pp 111–12.

24 Mac Niocaill, 'Irish "Charters"', p. 154.

25 Ibid.

26 O'Donovan, 'Irish charters in the Book
of Kells'; Mac Niocaill, *Notitiae as
Leabhar Cheanannais*; Mac Niocaill, 'Irish
"Charters"'; and Bairbre Nic Aongusa,
'The charters in the Book of Kells: a
historical analysis' (MPhil, University
College Dublin, 1989), pp 87–104.

27 Mac Niocaill, 'Irish "Charters"', p. 154.

28 O'Donovan, 'Irish charters in the Book
of Kells', pp 150–1.

29 Ibid., p. 151.

30 These are edited, translated and discussed
in Marie Therese Flanagan (ed. and
trans.), *Irish royal charters: texts and contexts*
(Oxford, 2005).

31 O'Donovan, 'Irish charters in the Book
of Kells', p. 152. For an edition and
translation of the *Additamenta*, see Bieler,
Patrician texts, pp 166–79.

32 O'Donovan, 'Irish charters in the Book
of Kells', p. 152.

33 James F. Kenney, *The sources for the early
history of Ireland 1: ecclesiastical* (New York,
1929), p. 5.

34 Mac Niocaill, *Notitiae as Leabhar Cheanannais*, p. 6.
35 Ibid., p. 7.
36 Mac Niocaill, 'Irish "Charters"', p. 153, n. 1.
37 Mac Niocaill, *Notitiae as Leabhar Cheanannais*, pp 1–2 and 'Irish "Charters"', p. 153.
38 Wendy Davies, 'The Latin charter-tradition in western Britain, Brittany and Ireland in the early medieval period' in Dorothy Whitelock, Rosamond McKitterick and David Dumville (eds), *Ireland in early mediaeval Europe: studies in memory of Kathleen Hughes* (Cambridge, 1982), pp 258–80.
39 Flanagan, *Irish royal charters*, p. 13, n. 26.
40 Kathleen Hughes, 'The Celtic church: is this a valid concept?', *Cambridge Medieval Celtic Studies*, 1 (1981), 1–20.
41 Broun, *Charters of Gaelic Scotland and Ireland*, pp 38–40 and 'The writing of charters in Scotland and Ireland in the twelfth century' in Karl Heidecker (ed.), *Charters and the use of the written word in medieval society* (Turnhout, 2000), pp 115–17.
42 Máire Herbert, 'Before charters? Property records in pre-Anglo-Norman Ireland' in Marie Therese Flanagan and Judith A. Green (eds), *Charters and charter scholarship in Britain and Ireland* (Basingstoke, 2005), pp 107–19.
43 Flanagan, *Irish royal charters*, pp 7–24.
44 Herbert, 'Before charters?', pp 107–8.
45 Flanagan, *Irish royal charters*, p. 13. For her discussion of the *notitiae*, see ibid., pp 13–23.
46 Mary Valante has argued that there exist other *notitiae* within the annals, specifically related to Connacht: 'Notitiae in the Irish annals', *Eolas: the Journal of the American Society of Irish Medieval Studies*, 1 (2006), 71–96.
47 Nic Aongusa, 'The charters in the Book of Kells' and 'The monastic hierarchy in twelfth-century Ireland'.
48 Herbert, 'Charter material from Kells'.
49 Casey, 'Studies in the exercise of royal power', '"A man of great power for a long time"', and 'Tigernán Ua Ruairc and the Book of Kells'.
50 On the concept of a 'monastic town', see also the second chapter in this book.

51 Herbert, 'Charter material from Kells', p. 63.

4. TIGERNÁN UA RUAIRC'S GRANT OF MAG nDECHRAD TO KELLS

1 Mac Niocaill, 'Irish "Charters"', pp 160-1 (§8(ii)). I have slightly adjusted Mac Niocaill's translation and standardized proper and placenames.
2 Although *cetna* appears interlineally in Royal Irish Academy A v 3, it is also found in the text of British Library Add. 4791, which suggests that the archetype(s) from which these two manuscripts were copied also considered the grants to have been related.
3 Mac Niocaill, 'Irish "Charters"', p. 154.
4 *ATig* 1039.3 and *CS s.a.* 1039.
5 *AU* 1046.2, *AI* 1046.6, *ATig* 1046.3, *CS s.a.* 1046 and *AFM s.a.* 1046.
6 *ATig* 1047.4.
7 *ATig* 1059.6 and *CS s.a.* 1059. It may be taken as an indication of the confusion (or deliberate obfuscation) of Uí Ruairc pedigrees that, although Cathal is described as a 'son of Tigernán, son of Níall, son of Áed Ua Ruairc' in the Annals of Tigernach, it is not possible to locate him in the Uí Ruairc genealogies.
8 *ATig* 1084.3.
9 *ATig* 1122.1 and *CS s.a.* 1122.
10 Plummer, *Bethada náem nÉrenn*, i, pp 36–7 and ii, p. 36 (§65).
11 *AI* 1095.11.
12 *ATig* 1114.4 and *CS s.a.* 1114.
13 Diarmuid Ó Murchadha, *The annals of Tigernach: index of names* (London and Dublin, 1997), *s.v.* Conmaicne.
14 *AU* 1122.1, *AFM s.a.* 1122 and *ALC s.a.* 1122.
15 F.J. Byrne, 'The trembling sod: Ireland in 1169' in Art Cosgrove (ed.), *A new history of Ireland, ii: medieval Ireland 1169–1534* (Oxford, 1993), p. 20. MacCotter suggests this movement was already taking place in the 10th and 11th centuries: MacCotter, *Medieval Ireland*, p. 221.
16 There were branches of Conmaicne scattered throughout Connacht and the midlands. One branch was located near the Uí Briúin homeland of Mag nAí, but they do not appear to have achieved any lasting place in history: Byrne, *Irish kings and high-kings*, p. 236.

17 For this latter expansion, see the discussion of Trácht Eothaile below.
18 Mac Niocaill, *Notitiae as Leabhar Cheanannais*, p. 25, n. 13.
19 MacCotter, *Medieval Ireland*, p. 219.
20 See, for example, the genealogies of Conmaicne Réin: Hennessy and Kelly, *The Book of Fenagh*, pp 385–7.
21 Mac Niocaill, 'Irish "Charters"', p. 159 (§6).
22 *ATig* 1029.2.
23 Byrne, 'Trembling sod', p. 15.
24 Keating, *Foras feasa ar Éirinn*, iii, pp 302–3.
25 Ibid.
26 *ATig* 1124.3.
27 *AU* 1129.5. For a map of the fortifications of Tairdelbach and Ruaidrí Ua Conchobair, see Donnchadh Ó Corráin, *Ireland before the Normans* (Dublin, 1972), p. 156.
28 *AU* 1004.7.
29 Myles Dillon (ed. and trans.), 'The taboos of the kings of Ireland', *Proceedings of the Royal Irish Academy*, 54C (1951), 8–11. Of the five identifiable *buada*, only one, *mílrath Náissi nó Maisten* ('the hares of Naas or Maistiu'), was from territory the Southern Uí Néill never possessed.
30 *AFM s.a.* 1022.
31 *ATig* 1172.8 and *AFM s.a.* 1172.
32 Ó Murchadha, *Annals of Tigernach: index of names*, *s.v.* Droichet Átha.
33 J.H. Andrews, 'The geographical element in Irish history' in *NHI, i*, p. 18.
34 *AU* 1084.4, *AFM s.a.* 1084 and *ALC s.a.* 1084. For this alliance, see Flanagan, 'High-kings with opposition', p. 901.
35 *AI* 1125.6, *AU* 1125.4, *ATig* 1125.7, *AFM s.a.* 1125 and *ALC s.a.* 1125.
36 Byrne, 'Trembling sod', pp 15–16 and Flanagan, 'High-kings with opposition', pp 923–4.
37 *AFM s.a.* 1133, *ALC s.a.* 1133, *Misc* 1136.1. Muirchertach Mac Lochlainn appears to have subsequently granted Findabair na nIngen to the monastery of Mellifont (*AFM s.a.* 1157). Doubtlessly he did so to express his suzerainty over Uí Cherbaill and possibly Uí Maíl Shechnaill too.
38 *AFM s.a.* 1136.
39 *AFM s.a.* 1135, 1136 and 1138.
40 *ATig* 1136.10 and *Misc* 1139.2. For *Bregnechaib* in the CELT version of the Annals of Tigernach, read *Brefnechaib*, as in the printed versions.
41 Brendan Smith, *Colonisation and conquest in medieval Ireland: the English in Louth, 1170–1330* (Cambridge, 1999), p. 21.
42 Keating, *Foras feasa ar Éirinn*, iii, pp 298–9.
43 Aubrey Gwynn and R. Neville Hadcock, *Medieval religious houses: Ireland* (Dublin, 1970), p. 195. It was certainly in existence before the death of Máel Caemgin Ua Gormáin, the Augustinian abbot of Termonfeckin: *AFM s.a.* 1164.
44 Mac Niocaill, 'Irish "Charters"', pp 160–1 (§8(i)).
45 Plummer, *Bethada náem nÉrenn*, i, p. 246 and ii, pp 239 (§198).
46 Muireann Ní Bhrolcháin, 'The manuscript tradition of the *Banshenchas*', *Ériu*, 33 (1982), 110. Charles Doherty, 'The transmission of the cult of Máedhóg' in Próinséas Ní Chatháin and Michael Richter (eds), *Ireland and Europe in the early middle ages: texts and transmission* (Dublin, 2002), p. 279.
47 *ATig* 1143.4; *AFM s.a.* 1153; *ATig* 1155.2 and *AFM s.a.* 1155; *AU² s.a.* 1159, *AFM s.a.* 1159; *AClon s.a.* 1160. The exception is *ALC s.a.* 1186: *Ro pho lán, dona, Midhi o Sinainn co fairci do chaislenaiph ocus do Galloibh* ('Mide, from the Shannon to the sea, was full of castles and of Foreigners').
48 James Carney (ed.), *Topographical poems by Seaán Mór Ó Dubhagáin and Giolla-na-Naomh Ó hUidhrín* (Dublin, 1943), p. 6.
49 F.J. Byrne, 'Monastica et onomastica', *Peritia*, 2 (1983), 264.
50 Tomás G. Ó Canann, 'Áth Uí Chanannáin and the toponymy of medieval Mide', *Ríocht na Mídhe*, 8 (1992–3), 80. Bieler, *Patrician texts*, pp 136–7 (§16).
51 Henry Savage Sweetman and Gustavus Frederick Handcock (trans), *Calendar of documents relating to Ireland, 1171–1301* (5 vols, London, 1875–86), v, p. 268.
52 Ó Canann, 'Áth Uí Chanannáin', 80.
53 Mac Niocaill, 'Irish "Charters"', p. 161.
54 *AU* 947.1 and *AFM s.a.* 945.
55 Ó Canann, 'Áth Uí Chanannáin', 81. The surname Ua Canannáin did not come

into existence before the middle of the 10th century: Tomás G. Ó Canann, 'Aspects of an early Irish surname: Ua Canannáin', *Studia Hibernica*, 27 (1993), 113–14 and 122–5.

56 Ó Muraíle cited in Ó Canann, 'Áth Uí Chanannáin', 83, n. 30.

57 Byrne, 'Monastica et onomastica', 264.

58 Ó Canann, 'Áth Uí Chanannáin', 80.

59 Keating, *Foras feasa ar Éirinn*, iii, pp 304–5. For a map, see T.W. Moody, F.X. Martin and F.J. Byrne (eds), *A new history of Ireland, ix: maps, genealogies, lists, a companion to Irish history* (Oxford, 1984), p. 26 (§24).

60 Mac Niocaill, 'Irish "Charters"', pp 156–7 (§3).

61 *Electronic Dictionary of the Irish Language*, s.v. *cetharaird* (http://www.dil.ie/8910) (accessed 2 July 2019).

62 *ATig* 1120.2 and 1120.4.

63 *ATig* 1101.8, *CS* s.a. 1101 and *AClon* s.a. 1100. The caveat F.J. Byrne offered with regard to using Edmund Hogan's *Onomasticon Goedelicum* holds true for the above discussion, namely that 'most territorial units changed their boundaries several times or disappeared from the political map altogether in the course of a thousand years': 'Monastica et onomastica', 261.

64 Mac Niocaill, 'Irish "Charters"', p. 161.

65 Ibid., p. 161, n. 56.

66 Ibid., p. 154.

67 For a discussion of the dating and location of the Synod of Kells see Aubrey Gwynn, 'The centenary of the Synod of Kells', *Irish Ecclesiastical Record*, 77 (1952), 161–76 and 250–64.

68 *ATig* 1152.2 and *AFM* s.a. 1152. Interestingly there does not appear to have been a major church at Droichet Átha at this period and Kells is first mentioned as a site of the synod by Keating: Gwynn, 'Centenary of the Synod of Kells', 165–7.

69 Donnchadh Ó Corráin, *The Irish church, its reform and the English invasion* (Dublin, 2017), p. 96.

70 H.J. Lawlor, 'A fresh authority for the Synod of Kells, 1152', *Proceedings of the Royal Irish Academy*, 36C (1921–4), 18.

71 Herbert, *Iona, Kells, and Derry*, pp 117–18.

72 Simms and Simms, *Kells*, p. 2.

73 *AFM* s.a. 1152. Keating, *Foras feasa ar Éirinn*, iii, pp 316–17.

74 Ó Corráin, *The Irish church*, p. 96.

75 *ATig* 1152.5 and *AFM* s.a. 1152.

76 Flanagan, *The transformation of the Irish church*, p. 183.

77 Ó Corráin, *Ireland before the Normans*, p. 161. As noted in the second chapter, Tigernán changed alliances approximately 16 times during his career. For an argument against seeing a rivalry between Ua Ruairc and Mac Murchada existing prior to 1152, see Denis Casey, 'Derbforgaill and the expulsion of Diarmait Mac Murchada', *History Ireland*, 27:3 (May/June 2019), 18–19.

78 *AFM* s.a. 1150 and 1152.

79 Diarmuid Ó Murchadha suggested that Bun Cuilinn is Bunkilleen, parish and barony of Mohill, Co. Leitrim: *Annals of Tigernach: index of names*, s.v. Bun Cuilinn. See also, Pádraig Ó Riain, Diarmuid Ó Murchadha and Kevin Murray (eds), *Historical dictionary of Gaelic placenames: fascicle 2 (Names in B–)* (London, 2005), s.v. Bun Cuilinn. Edmund Hogan thought that Bun Cuilinn was Daingen Bona Cuilinn in the parish of Kilmore, Co. Roscommon: *Onomasticon Goedelicum locorum et tribuum Hiberniae et Scotiae* (Dublin, 1910), s.v. Bun Cuilinn and Daingen Bona Cuilinn. If Hogan was correct then this would seem to support the previous argument for the location of Uí Ruairc vassals west of the Shannon in the vicinity of Mag nAí.

80 *ATig* 1152.6. Presumably this was Áed, whom the Annals of Tigernach called *in treas Aedh as fherr do bai a n-Erinn ina aimsir féin* ('one of the three best Áeds who was in Ireland in his own time'): *ATig* 1176.22.

81 *AFM* s.a. 1152.

82 *AFM* s.a. 1152. For the phrase *tar cenn*, see *Electronic Dictionary of the Irish Language*, s.v. *cenn* (http://www.dil. ie/8622) (accessed 2 July 2019).

83 *AFM* s.a. 1153. The Annals of Tigernach do not mention Ua Conchobair. They simply claim she fled from Laigin: *ATig* 1153.5. Neither *Expugnatio Hibernica* nor the *Song of Dermot and the Earl* records

her return: Scott and Martin, *Expugnatio Hibernica*, pp 24–7 (§1.1) and Mullally, *Deeds of the Normans in Ireland*, pp 53–9.

84 *AFM* s.a. 1153.

85 Mac Niocaill, 'Irish "Charters"', pp 154–5 (§1). For other general sanction clauses, see ibid., pp 155–62 (§§2, 4 and 9).

86 On contracts and sureties see Kelly, *Guide to early Irish law*, pp 158–76.

87 She suggests that 'grants to Kells by Tigernán Ua Ruairc, for instance, may first have been formalized in the areas in which the properties were situated, for both lay and clerical sureties came from his Bréifne lordship': 'Charter material from Kells', p. 71. It seems more likely, however, that the formalization occurred in Bréifne or Conmaicne since no Kells or Mide personages are mentioned.

88 On Muintir Maíl Mórda, see MacCotter, *Medieval Ireland*, p. 220.

89 Michael V. Duignan (ed. and trans.), 'The Uí Briúin Bréifne genealogies', *Journal of the Royal Society of Antiquaries of Ireland*, 64 (1934), 135–6 (§29–30).

90 *ATig* 1161.4.

91 *AFM* s.a. 1154; *ATig* 1155.11, *AFM* s.a. 1155 and *AU*² s.a. 1155; *AFM* s.a. 1161 and *AU*² s.a. 1161; *ATig* 1162.7.

92 Mac Niocaill, *Notitiae as Leabhar Cheanannais*, p. 26, n. 20.

93 *ATig* 1171.10. For evidence of Uí Ragallaig's alliance with the Anglo-Normans see Mullally, *Deeds of the Normans in Ireland*, pp 97–102.

94 Mac Niocaill, *Notitiae as Leabhar Cheanannais*, p. 26, n. 21.

95 *AU*² s.a. 1281 and *ALC* s.a. 1282.

96 Keating, *Foras feasa ar Éirinn*, iii, pp 316–17.

97 Pádraig Ó Riain, 'Sanctity and politics in Connacht *c.*1100: the case of St Fursa', *Cambridge Medieval Celtic Studies*, 17 (1989), 7–8.

98 Pádraig Ó Riain (ed.), *Corpus genealogiarum sanctorum Hiberniae* (Dublin, 1985), p. 51 (§315).

99 Whitley Stokes (ed. and trans.), 'Life of S. Féchín of Fore', *Revue Celtique*, 12 (1891), 331–53 (§§21, 24, 37–8 and 44–6). A 17th-century compilation of saints' genealogies makes him a descendant of

Áed Sláine: Paul Walsh (ed.), '*Genealogiae regum et sanctorum Hiberniae* by the Four Masters', *Archivium Hibernicum*, 6 (1917–18), Appendix 1, 54.

100 Rory Masterson, 'The diocese of Kilmore and the priory of Fore: 1000–1540', *Bréifne*, 10 (2003), 2.

101 Mac Niocaill, 'Irish "Charters"', p. 161, n. 56.

102 Ibid., pp 162–3 (§10).

103 Nic Aongusa, 'The monastic hierarchy in twelfth-century Ireland', 11–12.

104 Stokes, 'Life of S. Féchín of Fore', 320–3 (§§3–4) and 340–1 (§32).

105 *CGH*, p. 24.

106 Byrne, *Irish kings and high-kings*, pp 130 and 152.

1 Mac Niocaill, 'Irish "Charters"', pp 155–61 (§§2, 4, 8(i) and 8(ii)).

2 Ibid., pp 157–8 (§4). Mac Niocaill (followed by Herbert, 'Charter material from Kells', p. 62) suggested a date of between 1033 and 1049. However, if Máel Muire Ua hUchtáin was indeed *comarba* of Colum Cille, as an interlinear gloss suggests, then this *notitia* cannot date later than 1040, the year in which he died (*AU* 1040.2). Thus Nic Aongusa is correct in suggesting a date between 1033 and 1040: 'The charters in the Book of Kells', p. 83. Mac Niocaill's date of 1049 seems to be based on the obit of Amalgaid, abbot of Armagh (*AU* 1049.1), who is mentioned in the main text of the *notitia*.

3 Mac Niocaill, 'Irish "Charters"', pp 155–6 (§2).

4 Some of these issues are explored in Denis Casey, 'Dublin and the Gaelic Irish economy in the eleventh and twelfth centuries' in Seán Duffy (ed.), *Medieval Dublin XVIII: proceedings of the Friends of Medieval Dublin Symposium 2016* (forthcoming).

5 *AU* 1007.11. The phrase is found in an entry relating to the theft of the Book of Kells; on this see Denis Casey, 'An eleventh-century heist: stealing the Book of Kells', *Ríocht na Mídhe*, 31 (2020), 28–39.